S.T.A.R.S.

A Social Skills Training Guide for Teaching Assertiveness, Relationship Skills, and Sexual Awareness

SUSAN M. HEIGHWAY   SUSAN KIDD WEBSTER

Maine Coalition Against Sexual Assault
83 Western Ave, Suite 2
Augusta, ME 04330
(207)-626-0034

S.T.A.R.S.

A Social Skills Training Guide for Teaching Assertiveness, Relationship Skills, and Sexual Awareness

All marketing and publishing rights guaranteed to and reserved by

721 W. Abram Street
Arlington, Texas 76013
800-489-0727
817-277-0727
817-277-2270 (fax)
E-mail: info@FHautism.com
www.FHautism.com

Cover design and book layout: Matt Mitchell, www.mattmitchelldesign.com

ISBN 10: 1-932565-25-6

ISBN 13: 978-1-932565-25-6

Acknowledgments

Many colleagues and friends were involved in the completion of this guidebook. It is with deep gratitude that we extend our appreciation and thanks to:

- Marsha Shaw, for contributing a significant amount of energy and expertise in pilot-testing teaching techniques and in developing activities for each of the STARS content areas.

- Pat Patterson, who so willingly shared her expertise, inspiration and energy with us.

- Cathy Berger, who provided us with a tremendous amount of support.

- The production staff, including Patricia Mitchell, Yvonne Slusser, Leah Thompson, and Betsy True.

- Mariellen Kuehn of the Waisman Center; Jane Wittenmeyer, Howard Mandeville, Caroline Hoffman and other staff of the Wisconsin Council on Developmental Disabilities who were very supportive of our efforts over the years.

- Karen Maher and Don Anderson for assistance in publishing the 1998 edition.

- We are especially grateful to all of the participants in our training program, and their families and caregivers, from whom we have learned so much.

The Authors

Susan M. Heighway, MS, PNP-BC, APNP is a clinical professor and nurse practitioner with the University Center for Excellence in Disabilities, Waisman Center, and a Faculty Associate with the School of Nursing, University of Wisconsin-Madison. At the Waisman Center, she works as a nurse practitioner in two outpatient clinics serving people ranging in age from birth to adulthood who have developmental disabilities or genetic/metabolic disorders, along with those individuals' families. She is also the Nursing Discipline Coordinator for a federally funded Maternal and Child Health interdisciplinary leadership training program for graduate students.

Susan Kidd Webster, MSSW, LCSW is on the faculty of the School of Social Work, University of Wisconsin-Madison. For many years, she worked on capacity-building projects to support people with developmental disabilities in the community as an outreach specialist with the Waisman Center. Currently she teaches courses and coordinates training opportunities for undergraduate and graduate social work students focusing on people with developmental disabilities. She is also the parent of an adult son with cognitive disabilities.

Both Ms. Heighway and Ms. Webster have more than twenty years of experience in the area of sexual abuse prevention and sexuality education for people with developmental disabilities. They both served on a task force that was convened by the Wisconsin Council on Developmental Disabilities that addressed issues of sexual abuse of people with developmental disabilities. For several years, they worked together at the Waisman Center. They have provided consultation to community agencies, presented at conferences, gave guest lectures on campus, and conducted workshops on the local, state, and national levels regarding the areas of sexuality and sexual abuse.

Table of Contents

Section One

Introduction

How to Use This Book

Why Sexuality Education?

Misbeliefs and Facts About Sexuality and
Persons with Developmental Disabilities

Introduction

While we were providing clinical services, several adolescent girls with cognitive disabilities, who had experienced sexual abuse or who were considered to be at high risk for abuse, came to our attention at the Waisman Center, University of Wisconsin-Madison. In getting to know these eight girls, we discovered some common themes: self-doubt, non-assertiveness, loneliness, sadness about being "different," and confusion and discomfort about matters related to sexuality. These young women, all of whom had been through puberty, were surprisingly lacking in basic information about their anatomy and unique female body functions. We recognized, though, that these young women were also curious, social, desiring friends and other relationships, and eager to learn. As we attempted to link these girls with a community service that would meet their individual needs related to sexuality and abuse prevention, we could find none. The question, "Whose business is it?" would be one we would ask often. Believing in the need to create a resource where none existed, we began to make it our business.

From the start of our work, we realized the need for a clear definition of the term *human sexuality.* Our definition of the term encompasses a broad and complex spectrum of experiences and issues that includes the person's self-concept, sexual identity, sexual body functions, social interactions with the same or opposite sex, values and beliefs, sexual expression, sexual health, and future planning. Although we were not experts in sexuality education or sexual abuse prevention when we began, as instructors in social work and nursing, we did have basic knowledge of human sexuality, and experience working with persons with developmental disabilities. We also had a strong commitment to individual rights, including the rights of all persons to responsibly develop their sexuality and be safe from sexual abuse.

We continue to believe that with training and support, individuals with developmental disabilities can acquire the skills and knowledge necessary for developing a positive sexuality and reducing their risks for sexual abuse. This belief has been confirmed many times. In this guidebook, we hope to share with you our experience so that, working together, we can make it our business to be part of the solution rather than part of the problem.

> **Human sexuality refers to a broad and complex spectrum of experiences and issues, not only the physical act of intercourse.**

How to Use This Book

The purpose of this book is to share with you a model for teaching the concepts of human sexuality to people with developmental disabilities. The STARS model focuses on four content areas: Understanding Relationships, Social Interaction, Sexual Awareness, and Assertiveness, with the goals of promoting positive sexuality and preventing sexual abuse. We provide assessment tools that may be used for identifying the strengths and needs of each person for learning and support, in order to design an individualized training program. Goals and activities for each content area can be used to address these needs. This guidebook is intended for use by educators, social workers, nurses (and other health care providers), psychologists, residential/vocational support persons, family members, and others interested in assisting and supporting individuals in this sensitive area.

> For people with severe disabilities, who have limited capacity to learn self-protective behaviors, we believe that the ultimate responsibility for ensuring their safety and protection of personal safety needs to be assumed by trustworthy and sensitive caregivers.

The Activities

The activities in the guidebook are designed primarily for use with older teens and adults with mild/moderate developmental disabilities. Some of the concepts and activities, though, may be appropriate for younger children as well as adults with severe disabilities. For people with severe disabilities, who have limited capacity to learn self-protective behaviors, we believe that the ultimate responsibility for ensuring their safety and protection of personal rights needs to be assumed by trustworthy and sensitive caregivers. This book is to be used as an instructional guide rather than a packaged curriculum, and instructors are encouraged to decide for themselves which activities are most suitable, to make adaptations that meet the individual needs of the participants, and to enhance the training session with creative ideas.

Group or Individual

Most of the material in this book was developed out of our work with groups, but we have found that many of the activities and ideas can be easily adapted for individual training as well. When there are insufficient resources to support a group, the STARS activities can be used effectively in one-to-one training. For persons who do not learn well or do not desire to participate, individual training may even be preferred. For most people, though, a group experience provides the opportunity for social skills practice, peer modeling, and peer coaching, as well as the opportunity to meet new people and friends.

Why Sexuality Education?

Sexuality is an important part of the total life experience of human beings. As stated in the Introduction, our definition of human sexuality encompasses a broad and complex spectrum of experiences and issues that include the person's self concept, sexual identify, sexual body functions, social interactions with the same or opposite sex, values and beliefs, sexual expression, sexual health, and future planning. Not surprisingly, people with developmental disabilities have sexual feelings, needs, and experiences. As with most people, their sexual desires are often linked with needs for closeness, caring, and emotional intimacy with others. People with developmental disabilities have unique learning needs in many aspects of their lives—and sexuality is no exception. Individualized guidance and education for promoting positive sexuality and the prevention of sexual abuse is essential.

> "Prevention and education programs are important keys to reducing vulnerability to sexual abuse. Yet there is still a 'hit or miss' approach by those traditionally charged with teaching sexuality."
>
> —Case Manager

Sexuality education for most of us has been haphazard at best; some of our learning results from one or two classes in school, some from our parents, much more from our peers, and messages of all kinds from the media. For people with disabilities, opportunities for gaining accurate knowledge about sexuality may be even more limited. Many people with disabilities don't have access to books, health classes, or have the peer relationships in which positive attitudes and accurate knowledge can be obtained. Family members, community support providers, and others who support people with disabilities may be unsure of how much sexuality education to offer; they may be embarrassed to talk about sexuality, or they don't know how. As a result, many people with developmental disabilities lack basic sexual knowledge, are easily manipulated by others, and lack guidelines for the expression of sexual feelings.

It is important to teach people with disabilities appropriate information about human sexuality as well as sexual expression that fits their developmental needs. With today's emphasis on community inclusion, it is essential that we include comprehensive sexuality education and abuse prevention training in our support services. By providing appropriate education, training and support, it will be possible for people with developmental disabilities to develop the knowledge and skills that are necessary to engage in satisfying relationships and to acquire the protective behaviors necessary to move safely in society.

Misbeliefs and Facts About Sexuality and Persons with Developmental Disabilities

Misbeliefs and misunderstandings about sexuality and about people with disabilities can unnecessarily and drastically inhibit the sexual expression of those people. Misconceptions can also affect other areas of a person's life, including self-esteem, vocational performance, and motivation to live as independently as possible. Misbeliefs need to be dispelled and correct information needs to be provided.

> "However much we are cut off or sheltered from sex, however paralyzed or deformed we are, our sexual needs are the same as others."
>
> —Gunnel Enby,
> *Let There Be Love*

Misbeliefs Regarding Sexuality

- People with developmental disabilities do not have sexual feelings, or are asexual.

- People with developmental disabilities are over-sexed and have uncontrollable urges.

- It is unnecessary to talk about sex/sexuality because people with disabilities won't understand it, won't be able to cope with it emotionally, or won't have the opportunity.

Facts Regarding Sexuality

- People with developmental disabilities have a range of sexual desires and means of expression similar to that of people without a disability.

- The more accurate information and social skills training that people with disabilities receive, the more likely that their sexual behavior will be similar to the cultural norm.

Misbeliefs Regarding Sexual Abuse

People with developmental disabilities are not vulnerable to sexual assault because:

- People feel sorry for them or find them undesirable, so they will not hurt them.

- They spend their time in supervised or safe settings, so they are not exposed to dangerous or exploitative situations.

- They are not sexually active, so they are less vulnerable.

Facts Regarding Sexual Abuse

People with developmental disabilities may be more vulnerable to sexual assault for several reasons:

- They may lack basic knowledge about anatomy, intercourse (and other sexual activities), reproduction, and sexually transmitted infections.

- They may lack information/education about sexual abuse.

- They may have been socialized to be compliant, passive, and often exhibit a strong desire to please.

- They generally do not enjoy the same rights, privileges, and opportunities for privacy and normal healthy sexual relationships that most adults do.

The exploitation and misuse of accepted power relationships is a highly significant aspect of sexual assault. Offenders may think it is safer to assault someone with a disability because they perceive the individual as: unable to defend him/herself, unable to understand what is happening, unable to report the incident, or unlikely to be believed if he or she does report it.

An individual with a developmental disability may live, work, or spend leisure time in unsafe environments. A setting can be unsafe due to location, the structure, or occupants.

> **"The Seattle Rape Relief Project reported 700 cases of sexual abuse of persons with disabilities between 1977 and 1983. In over 90% of the cases the victim knew the perpetrator."**
>
> —Seattle Rape Relief Project, Seattle, WA

Section Two

The STARS Model

Skills
Training for
Assertiveness,
Relationship skills, and
Sexual Awareness

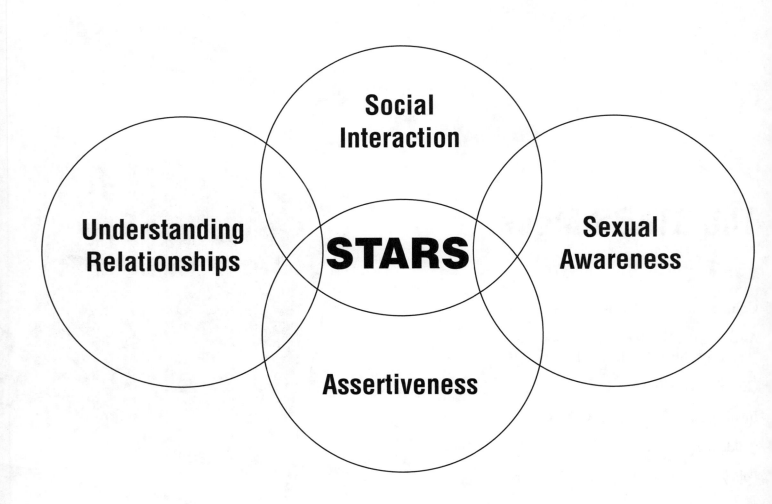

Social Interaction

Understanding Relationships

STARS

Sexual Awareness

Assertiveness

Content Areas and Goals

The STARS model originated through our efforts to design a training program for teaching basic personal safety skills to avoid sexual abuse. As we began working with individuals we quickly learned that the issues of sexual abuse were connected to other issues such as the person's self-esteem, assertiveness, understanding of sexuality, and opportunities to develop healthy relationships.

For people with developmental disabilities, we recognized the need to teach and support the positive expression of sexuality, in addition to facilitating the learning of skills to prevent sexual abuse. Equally important to consider in our work were the environments in which people spent their time; the attitudes and values of family, teachers, and caregivers; and the community's response at large. The realization of the complex issues people were facing led us to develop the STARS model, a training model more comprehensive and holistic than traditional methods.

In our STARS model, we present a "building blocks" approach to teaching individuals about sexuality and abuse prevention. The goals of the model are divided into four content areas. Each area offers unique concepts, which we then build upon in the next content area. For example, many of the activities in the Assertiveness section build upon skills acquired in all three of the other content areas.

The specific goals and activities in each area provide the necessary groundwork for the following area(s).

Understanding Relationships

- Building a positive self-image

- Identifying persons in one's life as family, friends, acquaintances, community helpers, and strangers

- Learning behaviors appropriate for each type of relationship

Social Interaction

- Approaching, responding to, and conversing with people in different settings and situations

- Expressing preferences, making choices

- Building friendships

- Engaging in mature relationships

- Recognizing options for relationships into adulthood

- Recognizing the components and responsibilities of a positive intimate relationship

- Understanding the responsibilities of parenthood and the pros and cons of having children

Sexual Awareness

- Building a positive self-image

- Identifying males and females

- Identifying body parts and understanding their functions

- Understanding public and private behavior

- Differentiating between inappropriate and appropriate touching

- Understanding the physical and emotional changes of puberty

- Understanding sexual feelings and behaviors

- Understanding reproduction

- Examining personal and societal norms and values regarding sexuality

- Learning about sexually transmitted infections

- Discussing other health issues related to sexuality

Assertiveness

- Increasing self-empowerment through words and actions

- Recognizing a situation as potentially unsafe

- Learning to say "no" and to use basic self-protection skills

- Knowing how and where to get help at home and in the community

- Reporting sexual exploitation or abuse

Assessing the Needs of the Individual or "Figuring Out What to Teach"

Before beginning the actual training with a group of individuals, we think it is necessary to assess each person's current knowledge, skills, and attitudes in the four content areas of the STARS model. We developed two assessment tools for this purpose, which are included in the Assessment section of this guidebook. The first, the Sexual Attitudes and Knowledge (S.A.K.) Assessment, is used to assess the participant's current knowledge and attitudes about sexuality and sexual abuse prevention. The second, the Sexual Abuse Risk Assessment (S.A.R.A.), is used to assess the person's life settings and relationship network for purposes of identifying factors and situations that may be increasing the person's risk for sexual abuse.

Along with use of the two assessment tools, interviews with the participant and significant others are also recommended to learn more about the person's unique concerns and needs, physical and social developmental levels, and cognitive functioning. It is essential to recognize the influence of a person's past experiences on their sexual attitudes, behaviors, and beliefs. A person's sexuality is influenced by experiences and guidance received from caregivers from early childhood across the life span. If a person experienced a family environment in which sexuality was supported in positive ways, then it is more likely that a sense of well-being and feelings of pride about one's body will develop. In contrast, a family that is uncomfortable with the subject of sexuality, makes negative comments about one's body, exhibits uncertainty or lack of information about sexuality, and expresses fear regarding the expression and control of sexual behavior, may impede healthy sexual development. The environment in which a person lives, including caregiver attitudes and beliefs, social opportunities, and social rules, can greatly influence the person's own sense of themselves as a sexual being.

The level of knowledge and experience related to sexuality and sexual abuse prevention may vary greatly for each individual, even for participants who are older adolescents and adults. Make no assumptions. Recognize, also, that incongruities might exist between the person's chronological age, social maturity, and physical

S.T.A.R.S. © 2008 by Susan Heighway and Susan Kidd Webster. Future Horizons, Inc.

development. For example, a person nineteen years of age who is fully developed physically, but whose cognitive abilities are more like a third-grader's, will need to have information adapted and presented at a level that he/she can understand.

Consider: What is the person's chronological age? Social maturity? Cognitive ability?

Are there any specific needs or concerns relating to sexuality that need to be addressed? Think about this in a comprehensive way. Here are just a few examples:

- Is the person interested in dating?

- Has the person had difficulties with sexually inappropriate interactions with others? With masturbation in public?

- Has the person been sexually assaulted? (If so, consider whether specific counseling from a mental health counselor might be necessary in addition to teaching sexuality information.)

The results of the two assessments, along with the interviews with the participant and significant others, can be used to determine where to focus training and support for each individual. The Individual Training Plan (at the end the Assessment section) can be used for each participant to record strengths/concerns, formulate plans for focusing the training/support/intervention, and to identify the persons responsible for carrying out the training.

Guidelines for Trainers

To be effective as a teacher, it is important to develop honest, open, and supportive relationships with the people whom you are teaching. To do this, you need to develop your own personal comfort level with the area of sexuality and with people who have developmental disabilities. Acceptance of individual difference, with objectivity, naturalness, and empathy is extremely important. Group participants will likely sense the feelings and attitudes of the instructor and, even if these feelings are not explicitly expressed, participants may internalize these beliefs. We have learned that if the instructor generates enthusiasm, conveys empathy, warmth, naturalness, and feelings of comfort, then a positive relationship is more likely to develop with the participants. To develop personal comfort and enhance group communication, it is helpful to consider the following principles:

- Examine your own attitudes about sexuality in general, and about sexuality and disability in particular.

- Foster a positive attitude about sexual feelings when providing sexuality information. The goal is to promote healthy sexuality and safety, not to eliminate sexual responses.

- Work toward becoming an "askable" adult regarding sexuality. Promote a positive atmosphere for learning by being flexible, honest, and direct in manner and speech.

- Listen carefully to everything a person says; listen towards understanding. Avoid being critical or overly judgmental so those participants feel they can share ideas and ask questions without fear or punishment.

- Acknowledge every individual's right to knowledge, privacy, and sexual expression based on personal orientation and decision, and advocate for this right.

- Be aware of the wide variety of behaviors, attitudes, and feelings related to sexuality, and deal with them in a sensitive manner.

- Provide accurate information about sexuality. Even if a person never asks any questions about sexuality, realize that the person has already acquired some information from other sources and needs to know that you will clear up misconceptions, distortions, and fantasies. Provide straightforward, correct information, and check the person's understanding in a supportive manner.

- Recognize that teaching a person about sexuality will not lead the person to act out sexual behaviors. Instead, understand that providing accurate, clear-cut information about sexual feelings and the physical aspects of sexuality will reduce confusion and minimize the risk of inappropriate behavior and vulnerability.

- Keep a sense of humor, while remaining respectful.

- Recognize that supporting and teaching individuals about sexuality can be challenging and stressful. Often, a network of support—even one or two others whom you can trust to be supportive—can help you cope with the stresses of providing education and support in this sensitive area.

Promote a positive atmosphere for learning by being flexible, honest, and direct in manner and speech.

Involvement of Significant Others

As we help people with developmental disabilities develop skills that will help them attain fulfilling lives, an important part of the training includes a focus on skills related to self-protection and the expression of positive sexuality. Within the individual's support network, a variety of persons—perhaps paid service providers, family members, or legal guardians—may be willing to take responsibility for ensuring these issues are addressed. To provide the most effective support, significant others need to be comfortable and knowledgeable in educating and/or responding to the person in regards to sexuality. Information and training to increase the comfort level and knowledge about human sexuality may be necessary and beneficial for these supportive individuals. The determination of which and how many significant others need to be involved in the training must be balanced by the individual's need for support and her/his rights of privacy and confidentiality.

We recommend that, prior to the start of the training program, you share information about the content and teaching methods with significant others. This allows time for questions and concerns to be shared and an opportunity to involve significant others in the training program. Sharing information can be done in a group or with individuals.

Many people wonder how sexuality training is received by the significant others in a participant's life. Our experience has been that most significant others realize that information on sexuality and the prevention of sexual abuse is vital to the person for whom they advocate. Most have welcomed our assistance in these sensitive areas and have been supportive to us in carrying out the goals of the training program. We have encountered a few people who were either uncomfortable with the idea of a sexuality training program or who withdrew the participant once the group got started. Some were not opposed to the training in general but were uncomfortable with specific content. In these situations we discussed concerns, provided information about specific components of the program, and came to an agreement about the individual's level of participation in the group. For people who were uncomfortable with the idea of a sexuality training program, sometimes we presented concerns in a non-threatening way about sexual abuse prevention and emphasized the importance of safety for the individual. Often, this opened the dialogue to other issues about sexuality education.

S.T.A.R.S. © 2008 by Susan Heighway and Susan Kidd Webster. Future Horizons, Inc.

Guidelines for Training

Group or Individual Learning

Most of the material in this book was developed out of our work with groups, but we find many of the activities and ideas suited or easily adapted for individual training as well. When there are not sufficient resources to support a group, the STARS activities can be used effectively in one-to-one training. For persons who do not learn well within a group or who may not want a group experience, individual training may even be preferred. For most people, though, the advantages of group participation are significant. The group provides the opportunity for social skill practice, peer modeling, and peer coaching, as well as the opportunity to meet new people and make new friends.

Facilitators

Learning in groups occurs most effectively when facilitated by at least two trainers. Co-facilitation is important so presenters can provide support to each other, to allow for adequate support to participation, and to monitor group dynamics. For co-educational groups, including both a male and female facilitator works best. It is important for facilitators to encourage active participation of all individuals. The instructors serve as models for the rest of the group by encouraging and listening carefully to each group member. Members who are less vocal are encouraged to participate. If concepts are raised that are not relevant to the topic, a respectful acceptance and gentle redirection is important. Each individual is reinforced for their efforts to contribute to the group.

Working with a Group: Selecting Participants

Who?

The original STARS activities were designed primarily for group work with older teens and adults with mild/moderate developmental disabilities.

Co-ed or not?

Groups can be co-educational or organized separately for men and women. We have found co-educational groups emulate the "real world" for most people. Co-ed groups enhance role-playing and other activities, as well as foster an appreciation for human development and sexuality issues of both sexes. The content area and/or the comfort level of the instructor may influence whether the instruction is done for a co-ed group or not. Sometimes men and women may feel more comfortable learning some content separately, or the facilitator may be more at ease presenting gender-sensitive issues in same sex groups. If the facilitator is comfortable, even gender-sensitive issues like menstruation and condom use can be taught and discussed in a co-ed group. For example, both males and females can benefit from learning about and actually handling menstrual hygiene products or condoms. Then, some of the more explicit discussion and demonstration about their use may be best done with same sex groups.

Number of participants in the group?

We recommend that the size of the group be small (4-8 members), so that the ratio of participants to facilitators will be about 2 (or 3) to 1. Size will depend on individual needs of the participants, learning styles, and capacity of group leaders.

Individuals with any type of disability?

People who have mild or moderate mental retardation, physical disabilities like cerebral palsy, hearing impairment, visual impairment, or behavior problems can participate in the groups. Consider whether a person will benefit from group participation. If the person has difficulty with disruptive behaviors when in a group setting, consider what types of support would be best so that the person can benefit from participation and so that others are not prevented from learning. Of course, needs must be individually assessed for each participant and training techniques modified accordingly.

Number & Frequency of Teaching Sessions

Sessions can be offered once a week for ten weeks and run approximately ninety minutes each, with a break. Other options include holding 45-minute sessions two times weekly for ten weeks. Information should be shared at a pace that is comfortable for the group or individual. The pace will vary with the capabilities, attention span, and learning style of the individual.

Sharing Information

Share information about your program with participants and significant others prior to beginning the training program. Help them understand the importance of the program, provide detailed information about the content and teaching methods, and obtain the support of significant others whenever possible. Some instructors offer to meet with significant others individually (with the permission of the participant) to review the content of the program and to promote continuity and reinforcement of the training in the home environment. Consider sending home a weekly summary of program lessons so that content can be addressed or reinforced at home and in the community with participants.

Selecting Content for Teaching

Select content and activities from this original STARS guidebook that have been identified as areas of need for the participants. When choosing content and activities, recognize that incongruities might exist between a person's chronological age, social maturity, and physical development.

For example:

- Consider a woman who is twenty-two years old, who is fully developed physically and who has a moderate cognitive disability. She has been fully included into community life with residential and vocational support, and she has the opportunities for many social experiences. Due to her cognitive disability, she has a very limited reading ability and difficulty with problem-solving and judgment.

- Consider a young man who is seventeen years old, who has Asperger's Syndrome and who is physically mature. He has high cognitive abilities, but he lacks awareness of the social world and he has limited skills for social interaction. His parents would especially like him to understand social relationships and appropriate behaviors so that he will be less vulnerable to sexual abuse.

The information and skills that both of these people need is very similar to those needed by other people their age, but the information that is provided to them will have to be adapted for their unique learning needs.

Choose content that will a) effectively reach the participants, and b) address issues relevant to their daily lives. For example, if a person works as a custodian in a shopping mall, and the job includes cleaning restrooms, it would be important to teach that person appropriate behaviors for respecting the privacy of others and for handling possible inappropriate sexual advances.

Instructional Methods

The method of training is as important as the content of training. Generally, the information about sexuality that is appropriate for people with disabilities will be the same information as for people without disabilities. For a person with a cognitive disability, information needs to be presented in simpler words, at a slower pace, and with much repetition, often aided by simple drawings or pictures.

Use a multi-sensory approach

We suggest that a variety of instructional methods be used. These methods include individual and group instruction, simple workbook activities, art, group discussion, audiovisual presentations, and role-playing. Anatomical dolls, slides, photographs, and line drawings are the effective methods for identifying reproductive body parts, describing body functions, and explaining the transmission of STDs. Group discussion, question-and-answer sessions, and storytelling are the most effective techniques for problem solving. Social skills are best taught through "real-life practice" role-playing, followed by group discussion. Lecturing is the least effective method because the group members may lose interest if not actively engaged.

Use your own creative methods for teaching

For some activities in the guidebook, there may be reference to specific resources (e.g., slides). However, effective teaching can happen just as well even if you do not have access to slides, fancy pictures, or anatomically correct dolls. Some of the best teaching tools are ones that are creatively made using common materials and that are tailored to the group or individual needs. We encourage enhancing your training sessions with your own creative ideas.

S.T.A.R.S. © 2008 by Susan Heighway and Susan Kidd Webster. Future Horizons, Inc.

- Consider using *The Social Skills Picture Book* and/or *The Social Skills Picture Book for High School and Beyond* by Jed Baker, which provide a visual learning format for learning social skills that apply to real-life situations. Both have CD-ROM versions available as well, which allow instructors to create custom slideshow presentations for groups, and/or print visual tools that students can take home.

- Consider using *The New Social Story Book* and *Comic Strip Conversations* by Carol Gray. These resources were developed for teaching social and communication skills to students in a wide variety of situations. They are great tools for teaching positive social skills and promoting a better understanding of the social world. Activities in this guidebook can be adapted to this type of formatting, particularly for individuals who have a good mastery of language. (See the Resources section for more information.)

Role-playing

Role-playing is a particularly effective technique because it involves active participation of the group members. It gives the participants an opportunity to try out and rehearse new behaviors and to identify and change inappropriate behaviors. Group members can take turns between acting and observing each other. The group facilitators often need to model and provide specific instructions and support to do the role-plays. The participants who are the observers can act as peer coaches and provide feedback to the role players. This active participation provides an opportunity for everyone to learn the concepts portrayed in the role-plays.

A potential drawback of role-playing is that, at times, role-plays can become too "real" for some participants. For example, when someone is acting out a situation where one person is angry, the participant may believe that the other person is genuinely angry. When role-playing a threatening situation, the participant may forget that they are acting, and may become truly frightened. It is important to keep reminding group members that "this is only acting, or make-believe." Another drawback could be that role-players might get too caught up in the fun of the role-playing, and work at being good actors rather than focusing on learning the concepts being taught. If the group facilitators provide ongoing sensitive support and instruction during the role-plays, the participants are less likely to experience these drawbacks.

Activities in the Natural Setting

Participants benefit most from the training when time is spent in their natural settings reviewing content and practicing skills related to the sexuality education training program. If trainers are not available for this individual work, other persons in the participant's support network could carry out this training activity. This time can be used to practice and reinforce skills and knowledge covered in the group meeting and to focus on issues identified in the Individual Training Plan. At the end of the Activities section for each of the four content areas, we have included Community and Informal Activities.

Periodically Reassess Learning

Periodically assess the progress of the individual or group, as well as the effectiveness of your instructional techniques. Do this by observing how well each participant can answer questions pertaining to the material (e.g., accurately labeling body parts), how well they join in group discussions about content, or how they participate in role-plays. Note also how the group responds to different methods of instruction (e.g., observing length of attention span, expressions of boredom, amount of fidgeting, level of interest, and enthusiasm) for determining the best teaching techniques. Modify content or teaching methods according to the needs, preferences and skills of the participants and your observations of their participation. The Sexual Attitudes and Knowledge (S.A.K.) Assessment tool may be used as a pre-test and post-test to evaluate learning of group members.

> "The most successful inclusion into society occurs when the individual develops skills for living in a sexually integrated world."
>
> —Counselor

Policy Implications for Service Providers

We find that our participants' behaviors and attitudes related to sexuality are influenced by service providers' policies regarding sexuality. The absence of a policy on sexuality also affects sexual expression. Adults with disabilities have the right to exercise their own choices and decision-making, and they have the right to social opportunities.

We encourage service providers to develop policies around sexuality and to make sure staff and consumers are aware of them. In the following excerpt from *The Right to Grow Up,* author Nancy Gardner provides an excellent discussion of these issues. [Where appropriate, content in the excerpt has been updated to reflect current philosophy and practice.]

> **Adults with disabilities have the right to exercise their own choices and decision-making and they have the right to social opportunities.**

The key to successful programs is provision of whatever services a particular individual needs to "make it" in her or his community and to do so in a way that is as much like what everyone else does as is possible. How "making it" is defined differs from culture to culture, town to town, family to family, even person to person. But some generalizations are possible. For example, almost everyone wants a comfortable home of his or her choosing; an enjoyable job that provides an adequate income to survive; and a loving, caring relationship with someone special, whether family, spouse, or friends. For most adults, the primary relationship in their life is with a sexual partner whom they have chosen as a mate.

When setting up services for persons with developmental disabilities, these same cultural goals should be considered. Generally, programs should have specific policies that encourage adult dignity and respect for the sexuality of the persons served. All service providers should ask themselves whether their policies take the following factors into consideration: privacy, social opportunities, respect for choice and sexuality, and protection of legal rights.

The rule of thumb for program policies should be to provide the same level of respect, privacy, and social opportunities that persons without disabilities expect in their own homes, workplaces, and communities.

Privacy

Does the person have a bedroom of their own? If not, are there "private places" where he/she can go to interact with potential sexual partners or to be alone?

If there is a shared bathroom, are there rules respecting each person's privacy when he or she uses it?

Social Opportunities

Are there opportunities for social interaction with both sexes?

Are transportation services available after 5 p.m. and on weekends?

Does social skills training include dating, and does the person have the opportunity to date if he/she desires?

Is the person provided with age-appropriate recreation and social activities?

Respect for Choice and Sexuality

Are there rules regarding bedtime or can individuals choose their own bedtime?

Are individuals given the opportunity to shop for their own clothes?

Are adult women taught to purchase and use cosmetics?

May individuals choose their own roommates and decide where, and with whom, they would like to go for recreational activities?

Are staff given training and policy guidance to develop an accepting attitude toward the sexuality of persons with disabilities?

Can couples remain in the service program if they choose to marry?

Are individuals given training in sexuality, birth control, avoidance of sexual exploitation, and interpersonal aspects of sexuality?

Are there specific procedures and policies regarding correction of inappropriate sexual behavior?

Are individuals provided with due process guarantees in regard to any training programs?

Are staff and parents given information about laws and policies, and medical and psychological consequences of sterilization?

Are there procedures for reporting sexual abuse, and policies relating to staff or others who may be involved?

Unfortunately, many programs have practices and patronizing policies that would be unthinkable for nondisabled persons. The rule of thumb for program policies should be to provide the same kind of respect, privacy, and social opportunities that persons without disabilities expect in their own homes, workplaces, and communities.

Reprinted with permission from Gardner, Nancy E.S., "Sexuality." In, Summers, Jean Ann (Ed.). (1986) *The Right to Grow Up*, Baltimore: Paul H. Brookes Publishing Co.

Understanding Relationships

Building a Positive Self-Image

Identifying Persons in One's Life as Relatives, Friends, Acquaintances, Community Helpers, and Strangers

Learning Behaviors Appropriate for Each Type of Relationship

Understanding Relationships

Except for the hermit on the mountain, we all live our daily lives in a network of relationships. The ability to identify people as family members, intimate and close friends, acquaintances, community helpers, and strangers is based on several abstract concepts. Developing an understanding of relationships, along with the norms of behavior and social interaction, is a key component for adolescents and adults with disabilities to build satisfying relationships and protect themselves from abusive situations. To develop an understanding of these abstract concepts, many people with disabilities need direct instruction and practice.

When teaching this content area, it is important to remember several factors that often affect the lives of persons with developmental disabilities. While most of us choose with whom we will live, work, and spend our leisure time, people with developmental disabilities often have little opportunity to make these choices. They may rarely have the opportunity to be with family members or develop social and intimate relationships. They are often forced to share personal living space and experience daily life in relationships that have been arranged by others. Fortunately, for many, these arranged relationships evolve into friendships or an alternative family. Many persons with developmental disabilities, though, have a tenuous relationship network due to high staff turnover or frequent change of environments. When most of the people in a person's network are paid staff, this lack of continuity of relationships can be very stressful. Staff members often fulfill multiple roles, including counselor, supervisor, or friend. Not surprisingly, many people with developmental disabilities experience confusion when defining their relationships with staff. In the role of "client," many adults with developmental disabilities have relationships with their families and service providers characterized by an imbalance of power. Whether real or perceived, this imbalance affects the feelings and behaviors associated with the relationship, often resulting in a diminished sense of self.

In our work, we also need to focus our efforts on expanding social networks and promoting opportunities for meaningful relationships to develop. Supporting relationships may be the most important investment we make toward improving the quality of life for people with developmental disabilities.

> **While most of us choose with whom we will live, work, and spend our leisure time, people with developmental disabilities often have little opportunity to make these choices.**

GOAL 1: Building a Positive Self-Image

Activities

1. Get acquainted. Put a large sheet on the wall for each participant. Write a group member's name at the top of each page and ask the person to respond to simple questions such as:

   • What is your favorite food?

   • What sports or activities do you like?

   • Where would you like to go on vacation?

   Continue for each group member. Point out common interests, as well as individual differences between group members. (See Example A: My Likes, at the end of this section).

2. Group sharing. At the beginning of each meeting give each person an opportunity to tell something of importance or interest that occurred during the week. It can be personal (e.g., "I have a new boyfriend") or general (e.g., "I got a new job"). Use this time to build group rapport. Acknowledge and accept all comments. If someone brings up something too sensitive for group sharing, tell him or her so, and suggest they talk with you or a support person in private.

3. Have each person think about when she/he is proud of or pleased with him/herself. Each person in turn can complete the sentence, "I am proud of myself when ..."

4. Share with individuals that how we feel about ourselves involves both things we can see on the "outside" and things in our mind or "inside." List things we can see on the outside (our physical appearance), and things in our mind or inside (our beliefs and feelings).

5. Make a booklet in the shape of a male or female with lines for writing. On the front or "outside," have participants list the things people can see which they like about themselves (physical self). On the "inside" of the book list things

they like about themselves which can't be seen (traits of their emotional selves, such as cheerful, honest, helpful, friendly).

6. Sitting in a circle, take turns having group members look at the person on their right and say something they like or find attractive about the person. This activity builds self-esteem, provides an opportunity to express opinions, and establishes a good time to practice accepting compliments in a gracious manner (saying "thank you" instead of giggling).

7. Using a full-length mirror, encourage each group member to look at his or her whole body. This helps the person with disabilities develop a concept and acceptance of their body boundaries and appearance.

GOAL 2: Identifying Persons in One's Life as Relatives, Friends, Acquaintances, Community Helpers, and Strangers

Activities

1. Have each group member bring a photograph of him/herself to the next group meeting. Make a poster by pasting each person's picture on a separate, large piece of paper to be displayed on the wall. In turn, have each person write the names of their close family members on the paper. Continue with each type of relationship from family members to close friends, co-workers, neighbors, community helpers, and strangers. (See Example B: Relationships, at the end of this section.)

2. Use *CIRCLES, Level I: Intimacy and Relationships*, Part I: Social Distance (see the Resources section) to illustrate relationships and social distance. This is a teaching tool designed to help youths with cognitive limitations and difficulties with abstract concepts grasp the idea of personal space, social distance, and appropriate social/sexual behavior. It teaches social distance and levels of familiarity through the use of colored concentric circles. We recommend using this tool in all settings where the student spends time so that she/he will be able to practice positive social behaviors specific for each setting. Learning positive social behaviors helps the student to be successful in social interactions with others, to decrease vulnerability and prevent sexual abuse.

First show the entire program on the video. Next, go through each type of relationship separately, addressing questions to the individual or group members. This gives the trainer an opportunity to make each area personally relevant to each individual. This also helps the trainer gain insight into the level of understanding of the group members and to identify areas that need extra attention. It is helpful to give each participant her/his own paper with the concentric circles. Some participants may learn better with pictures of people in their life in each circle.

3. "What is a family?" Discuss all types of families (e.g., families headed by two parents, single parents, foster parents, grandparents raising grandchildren, and same-sex parents).

4. Group discussion: "Who are your friends?" and "What is a friend?" Ask participants to name a friend and tell why that person is a friend. On a wall poster, list reasons why we call people friends; e.g., "help each other." The focus here is on understanding who our friends are and what friendship means. See the section on Social Interaction for activities related to how to make and socialize with friends.

5. Discuss other aspects of friendship. Points to emphasize:

   • Difference between a close friend and a casual friend.

   • Friendships often take time to develop. Have group members discuss any long-time friends.

   • Friends may not get along every day.

   • Friends change and it is okay to stop being friends if a relationship feels bad most of the time.

6. Define acquaintances: people whose names we know or recognize but are not as close to us as family or friends. Examples might include some neighbors, a store clerk or co-workers at your job.

7. Talk about strangers. Define stranger: anyone you do not know and whose name you do not know.

S.T.A.R.S. © 2008 by Susan Heighway and Susan Kidd Webster. Future Horizons, Inc.

8. Help group members identify who is or is not a stranger. Ask participants, by naming specific friends, family, and acquaintances, as well as strangers, to discriminate people they "know" from those they "don't know." For example, "Is the garbage collector a stranger? Is the librarian at the public library a stranger?" Review why people are or are not strangers.

9. Discuss types of strangers (people you do not know and whose names you do not know).

   • Safe strangers. These may include: (a) community helpers you could ask for help in an emergency, such as police, fire fighters, mail carriers, nurses; and (b) other people who live in our community, such as sales clerks, restaurant workers, other shoppers (especially women with children).

   • Dangerous strangers. These include people who want to harm others and from whom you want to protect yourself. Talk about clues that indicate someone may be dangerous. Include examples such as:

      » A stranger asks you to go somewhere with them or to get into their car.

      » A stranger offers to pay you money or give you a present if you do something that doesn't seem right.

10. Help participants use their intuition or "gut feelings" to identify possible dangerous or unsafe situations at home or in the community. Sometimes strangers hurt us, but other times even people we know may hurt us (touching our private parts, asking us to do something scary that we don't want to do, like touching their private parts). Discuss how your body feels when you are afraid or scared (stomachaches, heart pounds, breathe quickly, hands sweat). This means your body is telling you that something isn't right. Group members need to learn to respond to these feelings. Tell them not to talk to the person but to get away from him or her and tell a safe person. Protective behavior skills are more fully discussed in the section on Assertiveness.

11. Emphasize that most strangers will not harm you and that there are clues you can use (see Activity #10 in Goal #2, in this section, for this concept), and your "gut" feelings to help you tell if someone is dangerous.

GOAL 3: Learning Behaviors Appropriate for Each Type of Relationship

Activities

1. Use posters made earlier for each group member (see Activity #1 in Goal #2: Identifying Persons in One's Life, in this section) to review the people in their lives with their corresponding relationships. Identify the behaviors and patterns of interaction that are appropriate with each type of relationship and write the appropriate behavior under each relationship (See Example B: Greetings, at the end of this section.)

2. The "Is it okay?" Game. Read aloud the questions below about social behavior. Have participants respond to statements by holding up either a card which has OKAY or a card with NOT OKAY for each one. For example:

    *   Is it okay to kiss the store clerk?

    *   Is it okay to hug your mother?

    *   Is it okay to kiss your boss?

    *   Is it okay to hug someone you just met?

    *   Is it okay to wave to a stranger?

    *   Is it okay to give personal information to someone over the internet?

    Review these concepts in a discussion. Acknowledge that behavior sometimes depends on circumstances of where and when the interaction is taking place.

3. Role-play each different greeting used when meeting a friend, relative, co-worker, employer, or acquaintance.

4. On a large sheet of paper write down different behaviors such as kissing, hugging, shaking hands, and waving. Ask participants to list the people it would be all right to interact with in this way (e.g., mother, boyfriend). Continue listing

S.T.A.R.S. © 2008 by Susan Heighway and Susan Kidd Webster. Future Horizons, Inc.

people for each behavior. (See Example D: Who Would You …? at the end of this section.)

5. Use *CIRCLES, Level I: Intimacy and Relationships*, Part I: Social Distance (see the Resources section). This is a tool that illustrates social distance and can be used to identify the level of intimacy between people and pair it with the socially appropriate behavior for the relationship. Students will learn "relationship boundaries" and relationship specific behaviors (e.g., it's okay to hug your mother, it's not okay to hug the mailman).

First show the entire CIRCLES video. Next, go through each type of relationship and the appropriate behavior for that relationship. Address questions to each individual. This will give the trainer an opportunity to make each area personally relevant to each individual. It is helpful to give each participant his or her own paper with the concentric circles. Some participants may learn better with pictures of people in their life in each circle.

Community or Informal Activities

1. There are many opportunities to foster self-esteem on a daily basis in natural settings. Encourage participants and significant others to make positive statements when appropriate, such as, "John, I'm so glad to see you today," or "I noticed that you have a new haircut, Eve, and it looks very pretty on you."

2. Peer groups can be encouraged to reinforce each other. For example, by clapping for each other's successes, or making comments to each other using "I like it when you …" statements.

3. While in the community, ask the person to identify community helpers. Include "safe" people such as bus drivers, store clerks and teachers who might be approached if help is needed. Point out that police are not always around and it is important to identify who may be other "safe" people.

4. With the group member, look at his/her photo album. Identify specific people and discuss various types of relationships.

5. Watch a favorite TV show or movie together to identify relationships between the characters in the show and talk about their behavior—is it appropriate for their relationship or not?

Understanding Relationships – Activity Examples

Example A

My Likes—by Mark

Pizza, Summer, Bowling, Hawaii

Example B

Mark's Relationships

Paste photo of each person.

Joan - Mom

Mike - Best Friend

Ellen - Neighbor

Susan - Job Coach

S.T.A.R.S. © 2008 by Susan Heighway and Susan Kidd Webster. Future Horizons, Inc.

Example C

Greetings
Paste photo of each person.

Joan - Mom
Kiss

Mike - Best Friend
Hug

Ellen-Neighbor
Wave

Susan-Job Coach
Shake Hands

Example D

Who would you ... ?

Kiss	Parents, boyfriend
Shake Hands With	Someone being introduced to you
Hug	Good friend, family member
Wave At	Neighbor, child

Section Four

Social Interaction

Approaching, Responding to, and Conversing with People in Different Settings and Situations

Expressing Preferences, Making Choices

Building Friendships

Engaging in More Mature Relationships

Recognizing Options for Relationships into Adulthood

Recognizing the Components and Responsibilities of a Positive Intimate Relationship

Understanding the Responsibilities of Parenthood an the Pros and Cons of Having Children

Social Interaction

The opportunity for social interaction is important to all of us. To interact effectively with others, we learn how to approach people and respond to people in ways that are acceptable in our culture. As we are socialized, we learn to express our needs, preferences, and opinions, how to give and get information, and how to make friends and develop intimate relationships.

As people with developmental disabilities become more involved in community life, we realize that the need for social skills training is as important as instruction in cooking, money management, housekeeping, or shopping. Social skills are often acknowledged as important, yet given low priority when individual learning goals are written and carried out. As a result, many people lack the skills to effectively communicate their feelings and wishes; they are unable to positively relate to others. Some people may even develop inappropriate or anti-social behaviors that jeopardize their participation in educational and vocational programs.

Many people with developmental disabilities need specialized support and "coaching" for understanding social rules and developing socially appropriate behaviors. Direct instruction in social skills, positive role modeling, and lots of opportunity for practice can greatly enhance social integration of people with developmental disabilities.

Social adjustment is closely linked to self-esteem. The self-concept is also enhanced by opportunities to make choices, express preferences, and give opinions. The way we interact with others impacts our lives in many ways, affecting our abilities to protect ourselves from harmful situations and to develop satisfying relationships.

The goals and activities in this section build upon the group members' fundamental understanding of relationships and accompanying behaviors, which was covered in the Understanding Relationships section. Social skill development is excellent groundwork for the later section, Assertiveness.

> "We were strangers in her first year, 1986. Then we met. Then she transferred, same year. We met together. Closer. Did things. What would you like to do today? Let's go bowling. We planned it together. We held hands, hugged a lot. Because we were friends. As best friends."
>
> —Robert

GOAL 1: Approaching, Responding to, and Conversing with People in Different Settings and Situations

Activities

1. Who and where would you … ? On a large sheet of paper write the word MOTHER or someone you may kiss. Then list several settings—home, grocery store, ball game, restaurant. Ask if it is acceptable to kiss in all of these places or why not, and what other factors might be important (your age, presence of others, type of activity going on). Continue the activity for other people, behaviors and settings. (See Example E at the end of this section.) Discuss how behaviors or interactions differ according to the setting as well as the person.

2. Identify facial expressions and feelings. Show participants' various facial expressions and label the feelings that go along with them (e.g., angry, sad, and happy). Have group members make facial expressions also. Use of a mirror is helpful.

3. Role-play the expression of various feelings using words, signs, pictures, gestures, or expressions. For example, how would you express these feelings?

   • Sadness

   • Anger

   • Feeling sorry

   • Love

   Note: Some people who have cerebral palsy or similar disabilities that affect muscle movement have difficulty making their facial expression match their emotion. Be sensitive to possible frustration for these persons and assist them in developing alternate ways of communicating their emotions. For example, make use of symbols or pictures for feelings and emotions.

4. What is the Message? Role-play situations in which children are asked to figure out nonverbal communication. For example, what is the message if the person:

- Smiles and nods head? (Yes or okay)

- When greeting a person, extends arm and hand? (Wants to shake hands)

- Pulls body back when approached for hug? (Doesn't want to hug)

5. Role-plays. Once the group is comfortable with role-plays, ask them to suggest situations they would like to role-play. Here are two examples to begin:

- Meeting someone new at a party. Two people pretend to be at a party where they meet each other for the first time. Role-play introducing themselves to each other and making conversation. Point out appropriate amount of information to reveal and topics of conversation with someone you are meeting for the first time.

- Conflict resolution. Two participants role-play that they are coworkers who are having problems getting along with each other at work. Practice ways they can express their feelings to each other and resolve conflict.

GOAL 2: Expressing Preferences, Making Choices
Activities

1. Use Activity #1 in Goal #1: Building a Positive Self-Image, in the Understanding Relationships section, to help group members share interests and express preferences.

2. Show the group three pieces of artwork. Ask each person which one he/she likes the most and why? Discuss individual preferences or tastes. Ask what opportunity participants have to make choices (e.g., if they have choices in clothing, room decor, or activities).

3. Tell short stories in which the character must make a choice. Have each group make their own decision about what they would do and why. Examples of short stories:

- Cindy is planning to go bowling with friends. Her sister, Linda, calls and invites her to dinner the same night. What do you think she should do?

- Ron and his roommates are planning a picnic for Saturday. What do you think would be good to bring along to eat?

- Your coworkers have organized a roller skating party and invite you to come. You would really like to go but you feel embarrassed because you don't know how to skate. What are some of your choices? What would you choose to do?

- Your friend, John, tells you about a new social group forming and he invites you to join. Discuss what things you might want to consider when making your decision (e.g., the activities of the social group, the other group members attending, and the time of the meetings).

GOAL 3: Building Friendships

Activities

1. For activities about building friendships, see Activities #4 and #5 in Goal #2: Identifying Persons in One's Life, in the Understanding Relationships section. As a group, create a list of attributes to look for in a good friend. For example:

   - Likes to have fun

   - Likes to do things together

   - Listens to you

   - Really cares what happens to you

   - Stands up for you

   - Helps you when you are sick

2. Make a similar list of "ways to be a good friend."

3. Use *CIRCLES, Level I: Intimacy and Relationships*, Part II: Relationship Building (see the Resources section) to help students develop an understanding of how intimacy levels change as relationships change, e.g., an acquaintance who becomes a close friend.

   See Activity #2 in Goal #2, and Activity #5 in Goal #3, both in the Understanding Relationships section, for other activities using the CIRCLES program.

4. Ask the group to think of someone whom they would like to know better. Make a list of things they could do to become closer to the person. (See Example F: Ways to Become Better Friends, at the end of this section.) Role-play one or more of the suggestions.

5. Role-plays.

   • Your friend feels bad. What could you say or do?

   • Giving and receiving a gift.

   • A co-worker asks you to go the movies. You don't feel like going out tonight but you are interested in developing a friendship with the person. What could you say or do?

   • Inviting a friend to visit your home.

6. Review etiquette and manners. For example:

   • Saying good-bye.

   • Taking turns in conversations.

   • Saying "please" and "thank you."

   • Role-play situations involving various social skills and table manners.

7. Host a "gourmet" meal with group members. Encourage participants to practice manners at a table set with linens, flowers, and candles. Go out to a "nice"

restaurant. Practice ordering, using manners at the table, and conversation skills during the meal.

GOAL 4: Engaging in More Mature Relationships
Activities

1. Review the concept of respect as a necessary component in a good relationship. How do people show respect? How do you know someone respects you? Role-play showing respect.

2. Introduce "romantic" relationships. Explain that teenagers and adults sometimes have friendships that develop into romantic relationships—like between a husband and wife or two people who are dating. In a romantic relationship the person has special feelings for another, which are called being "in love." Have group members identify someone they know or someone in a movie or TV show that is in a romantic relationship.

3. What is love? Discuss the different types of love a person can have. For example, loving a pet, loving nature, loving people in your family, loving God, loving a good friend, married love (which can include being friends and sexual love).

4. What is the difference between "liking a person" and "loving a person"? Explain that the difference is related to how strong the feelings of affection and attraction are towards the other person. Have students draw someone or something they "like" and someone or something that they "love." Ask them to discuss their choices. Consider the following:

    •   If you are friends with someone, the relationship could just remain as a friendship, and you could become "really good friends."

    •   Sometimes when you meet or look at someone, you realize that you feel something besides friendship—you have "romantic" feelings. These feelings may turn into love—a really strong caring feeling. Love is more than physical attraction, a person's "inner qualities" are also important and it takes time for love to develop. Also talk about strong attraction before you really get to know the person well; it might not be love, but "infatuation."

S.T.A.R.S. © 2008 by Susan Heighway and Susan Kidd Webster. Future Horizons, Inc.

5. Discuss what happens when you think you care about someone:

   • Sometimes the other person will like you as much as you like them, or more, or less; or

   • Sometimes the other person will not be interested in a relationship with you; or

   • Sometimes your feelings could change (feelings get stronger or deeper, or less interested).

6. What do you look for in a boyfriend or girlfriend? Emphasize the "inner qualities" vs. the "outer" or surface qualities.

7. When people who have a romantic relationship go out together, it is called "dating." Note that you can also have a "date" with someone who is just a friend. Discuss each aspect of a date:

   • Planning the date—where, when, transportation, phone number, address, cost.

   • Asking someone—by phone, in person.

   • Accepting/refusing a date.

   • Getting ready—hygiene, appropriate dress.

   • Behavior on the date—saying good night.

   Role-play or help the group members plan actual dates and rehearse each aspect of the date. More content on dating behaviors and values is included in the Sexual Awareness section.

GOAL 5: Recognizing Options for Relationships into Adulthood

There are many options today for developing satisfying relationships in adulthood. Many people have connections with others that do not involve romantic relationships. It is important to help group members develop an awareness of the options available to them. All of us have the human need for feeling connected with other people, but this may come in different forms. Assist participants in considering which of the options would feel most satisfying for them. For some people, it might mean living with an adult foster family and having a few same-sex peers as close friends to share special activities. It might mean having a special opposite sex or same-sex romantic partner, perhaps headed toward living together and a more permanent relationship as in marriage, or not.

Activities

1. Help group members list several options for adult life. (Most likely the messages that most of us have gotten is that to be "okay," we need to be married and have children.) Encourage group members to consider a range of possible options for a satisfying life. Examples include living with a roommate, working at a job in the community and have a satisfying social life.

2. Give each participant a turn to think about what they would like in their future. Help them think about options for their future. Examples include living in an apartment, owning a house, having a job, having friends, and getting married. Take into consideration what responsibilities each of these require. People with disabilities may need support to accomplish their goals—help them think about what support they might need.

3. Create a story about independent living. In the story, include the responsibilities of living independently and managing a household. Include earning money, paying bills, and doing household tasks, cooking, shopping, and using transportation. Various group members may need different levels of support for these tasks. Assist individuals to develop an understanding of the complexity of independent living. An example of a story which might be used:

   - Ralph moved into an apartment last month. To pay for his expenses, he has a job and he receives government benefits that he is qualified for because he has a developmental disability. His expenses include rent, food, phone bill, bus fare, and clothing. A support worker from the agency responsible for his residential placement stops by daily after Ralph gets home from work to assist with food preparation, talk about Ralph's daily routine, and help in problem-solving Ralph's concerns and needs.

- List on a large sheet of paper or the blackboard the responsibilities in the story. If there are other things that Ralph would need to do in his household, list these too.

GOAL 6:   Recognizing the Components and Responsibilities of a Positive Intimate Relationship

Activities

1. Review the concepts of friendships and the qualities of a positive relationship, using Activity #4 in Goal #2: Identifying Persons in One's Life, in the Understanding Relationships section. Talk about the things outside (physical appearance) and the things inside (inner qualities) that make up a person. Remind participants that the "inner" qualities of a person are the most important to consider when deciding whether or not to have a relationship with someone and what kind of relationship it will be.

2. During group meeting, model, label, and reinforce behaviors and attitudes that promote friendship and relationship building.

3. Group discussion. Ask group participants for their ideas about the different stages or steps that two people go through together on their way to developing an intimate relationship and making a commitment to each other.

    - These steps include: becoming friends, dating, asking yourself if this is the right person for you, asking yourself if this is the right time to make a serious commitment, marriage, or partnership.

    - Emphasize that it is best if these steps take some time, rather than rushing into making a serious commitment. Help participants realize that on television and in the movies, couples seem to go through these steps or stages very quickly. But, in real life, it is better to get to know the person slowly and ask yourself each step of the way if this is the right person and decision for you.

- Review all of the steps. Talk about each step, listing it on a piece of large paper or on the blackboard. Underneath, list the specific activities that two people do in each step. For example, under "becoming friends" you might list, with the help of the participants, that you do things together and talk about things you have in common. Under "asking yourself if this is the right person for you," you might list, "identifying the inner qualities of the person."

- Discuss concepts with group members who may be in a particular stage of a relationship.

4. Role-play conflict resolution and problem solving. The ability to successfully resolve conflicts and solve problems when living with others requires the individual to avoid blame, name-calling, making judgments, and telling the other person what to do. Group members will benefit from practicing positive problem-solving behaviors to reach a satisfying resolution. Have participants suggest specific problem situations they have experienced with others. Group members can role-play behaviors to solve the problem in a positive way; then role-play behaviors that would prevent a positive solution to the problem. Discuss problem-solving strategies.

5. Group discussion about marriage. Ask group members some of the reasons why they think people get married. These reasons include love, companionship, sexual attraction, respect, mutual interest, mutual goals, mutual values, and the ability to communicate and solve problems. Then continue the discussion with some of the wrong reasons for getting married: just wanting to have sex, "everyone is getting married," pressure from friends/family, avoiding problems at home, or pregnancy.

6. Group discussion. Discuss positive reasons for making a long-term commitment. Review important aspects of a positive relationship. What does it feel like to love someone? How do people show love in different types of relationships? What do we mean by respect? How do people show respect in a committed relationship? How do you know when your partner respects you?

7. Create a story about a couple. In the story, include the responsibilities of a committed realtionship. Include the aspects of managing a household. Ex-

amples include earning money, sharing household tasks, cooking, shopping, finding time for recreation, and taking care of each other during sickness.

- Example: Alex and Heather got married six months ago and they rented an apartment. To pay rent and all their other expenses, such as food, the phone bill, and clothing, they both must work in the community. Heather likes to get up early each morning. While Heather fixes breakfast, Alex makes lunches for each of them to carry to work. Alex and Heather ride the bus together. Heather gets off the bus first at her job and she tells Alex she will see him in the afternoon. Alex gets off the bus at his job. After work, Alex and Heather ride the same bus home, but they stop at the grocery store on the way home to buy groceries. Heather doesn't feel very well when they arrive home, so Alex suggests that she go to bed and he fixes soup for them both.

- List on a large sheet of paper or the blackboard the responsibilities for the couple in the story and list who did each activity. For example:

  » Work in the community—both Heather and Alex

  » Fix breakfast—Heather

  » Grocery shopping—both Heather and Alex

  » Fix supper—Alex

Identify and list other things that Heather and Alex would need to do in their relationship and in their household.

GOAL 7: Understanding the Responsibilities of Parenthood and the Pros and Cons of Having Children

Activities

1. What must parents provide for a child in order to assure adequate care? Individually, or in a group, discuss the need for housing, food, clothing, health care, childcare, toys, education, and discipline. What do parents need to do to

provide these things for their children? Do your students think they are capable of raising children now, or ever? Talk about why and why not.

2. Role-play. Have two people take the roles of parent and young child. They role-play a situation in which the parent tries to find ways of getting the child to clean her room and the child does not want to do it. Afterwards, talk about the difficulty in getting the child to do the activity, and discuss what techniques the parent used to gain their child's cooperation. Be sure to reinforce positive parenting techniques.

3. Invite a young couple with a small child to share some of their experiences in learning about the responsibilities involved in marriage and starting a family.

4. Discuss other options, besides parenting, for interaction with children. Talk about roles, such as being an aunt/uncle and work or volunteer opportunities in a daycare setting or school. For the safety of all, encourage adults with disabilities to get permission from the child's parent to interact with them and do so in the presence of a parent.

5. Realistic exposure to daily life with children is important. For example, visit a daycare center so that group members can observe and spend time with children.

Community or Informal Activities

1. Encourage and provide opportunities for participants to make choices in their daily life (e.g., choosing activities, making purchases, picking out clothing, deciding what to eat). Making these choices gives individuals experience and preparation for making bigger decisions such as choosing friends or being sexual with another person.

2. Encourage participants to be involved with planning processes in which decisions are made about their own lives.

3. In natural settings, model, label, and reinforce behavior and attitudes toward people who promote friendship and relationship building. Prompt or coach people when they seem confused.

S.T.A.R.S. © 2008 by Susan Heighway and Susan Kidd Webster. Future Horizons, Inc.

4. When reading books or stories, or watching TV or videos, point out examples of friendship and relationship building.

5. Some communities have developed "Personals" sections for persons with disabilities in safe, supportive publications, such as newsletters. Placing or responding to "ads" can be a means of positive social networking. Help the person write and/or respond to ads and be sure to review safety precautions.

Social Interactions – Activity Examples

Example E

Mother (Kiss)

Home	Yes
Grocery Store	No
Movies	No
Picnic	Maybe

Example F

Ways to become friends

Eating lunch together

Inviting someone to my house or visiting their house

Talking to them on the phone after school or work

Going places together

Example G

A good friend:

Cares about me

Spends time with me

Is someone I can talk to about my problems

Is someone I can have fun with

Section Five

Sexual Awareness

Building a Positive Self-Image

Identifying Male and Female

Identifying Body Parts and Understanding Their Functions

Understanding Public and Private Behavior

Differentiating Between Inappropriate and Appropriate Touching

Understanding the Emotional and Physical Changes of Puberty

Understanding Sexual Feelings and Behaviors

Understanding Reproduction

Examining Societal Norms and Values Regarding Sexuality

Learning about Sexually Transmitted Diseases

Discussing Other Health Issues Related to Sexual Awareness

Sexual Awareness

Along with being social, we are sexual beings. From an early age, most of us began to discover our sexuality. As children, we wondered: Where do babies come from? Why don't girls have a penis? Will I get breasts when I grow up? How the people in our lives responded to the curiosity and provided information shaped our attitudes and behaviors about sexuality.

For most people, the desire for sexual knowledge and identity continues into adulthood as concerns naturally broaden to include issues of intimacy, fertility, sexual dysfunction, sexually transmitted diseases, and personal and societal values related to sexual expression. This includes people with developmental disabilities who may or may not actively seek information or ask questions about sexuality. In the past, support providers were often misguided and used excuses to avoid the topic of sex: "We think they won't understand. If they do, we are afraid what they will do with the knowledge." "We think their parents will get upset." "We are embarrassed to talk about it." "We don't know how to talk about sexuality." As a result, many adults with developmental disabilities lack basic sexual knowledge, are easily manipulated by others, and lack guidelines for the expression of sexual feelings.

Some of the young adults with whom we have worked have been taught to avoid sex because it is bad, something they shouldn't talk about, and certainly should not engage in. Other young persons we have encountered have been given no direction in regard to sexual expression. Their unacceptable behaviors have been excused by caregivers who believe that the person is incapable of learning otherwise or controlling him/herself.

Through our experiences, we have come to strongly believe that all individuals benefit from accurate information about human sexuality. Knowledge about the body and how it works heightens self-confidence, increases self-esteem, and allays misconceptions and fears. When we answer questions, discuss issues and give support and guidance, people with developmental disabilities are more likely to exercise self-control, master concepts, and make informed choices. If people with developmental disabilities develop an understanding of sexual feelings, there is a greater likelihood that sexuality will be expressed in acceptable and responsible ways, and that the risk of sexual abuse will be lessened.

> "Few people are forced to expose themselves in the nude so often as the physically disabled who can't look after their own hygiene... Your private parts are as depersonalized as yourself, they are washed and cleaned in a way regarded as natural for sick people; perhaps it is right, but the sexually deprived are forced to lie there exposed with expressionless faces hoping no one will notice what pleasure or disgust they are experiencing."
>
> —Gunnel Enby,
> *Let There Be Love*

GOAL 1:   Building a Positive Self-Image

Activities

1. Review the activities under Goal #1: Building a Positive Self-Image, in the Understanding Relationships section.

2. Ask each participant to (a) tell something that they like about how they look and (b) tell something that they would like to change, if they could.

3. Compare ourselves with others and accept our differences. Help participants identify eye color, facial characteristics, hair color and texture, and body type (e.g., tall or short) among the group. Note that everyone is different and each person is "okay." Perhaps someone in the group uses a wheelchair, has difficulty speaking, or is visually impaired—these are other examples of differences.

4. Discuss ways that we take care of ourselves and keep ourselves looking good.

    *   Include washing/bathing, eating healthy foods, brushing teeth, getting enough sleep, brushing or combing hair, and exercise/activity.

    *   List other things that people do to keep themselves looking good such as wearing makeup, wearing jewelry, going to the hair salon/barber shop, wearing braces on teeth, and keeping nails clean and manicured.

GOAL 2:   Identifying Male and Female

Activities

1. Have participants cut out pictures from magazines of males and females, and paste them on a piece of paper. Discuss female and male characteristics. Look at the pictures and discuss gender differences. Use this activity to dispel stereotypes and discuss uniqueness of individuals.

2. Help participants explore the roles and behavior of men and women in today's society. Use books and pictures to identify males and females in a variety of non-stereotypical roles. Talk about stereotypes such as "men don't cry," "only women take care of babies," and "men are doctors, women are teachers and nurses." Discuss how gender roles may be influenced by culture.

"I strongly believed that Pam was a victim, not because of her mental retardation, but because she did not know anything about sex."

—Counselor at a rape crisis center

S.T.A.R.S. © 2008 by Susan Heighway and Susan Kidd Webster. Future Horizons, Inc.

GOAL 3: Identifying Body Parts and Understanding Their Functions

It is important that people with disabilities feel as comfortable with identifying and labeling their sexual body parts as with any other body part. Knowing about one's whole body is important for a healthy self-concept. It is also important to have understandable words to be able to communicate to others about one's sexual parts. This includes using words to tell someone about being in pain or injured, about an experience of sexually abusive behavior, or to tell a partner what is pleasurable.

When teaching about body parts, it is best to use pictures or drawings that are clear and simple (see the Assessment section for examples of pictures). Show internal organs as they appear in the whole body, so the participants can visualize the location of the body part. Showing only a body part, as it looks separate from the body, may be confusing.

Activities

1. Review the location and function of non-sexual body parts using pictures, drawings, or anatomically correct dolls. Have the participants identify body parts in one or both of two ways: (1) point to the part and ask the person to name it, or (2) name the part and ask the person to point to it. Talk about the function of the body parts—for example, "What are arms used for?" "What are ears used for?" "What is the stomach for?" and so forth.

    *   Review external body parts (the parts of the body that we can see). Use the basic body parts (arms, legs, eyes, hair, and so forth) and don't become too detailed (avoid parts such as phalanges or palpebral fissures).

    *   Review internal body parts (those parts inside our bodies that we cannot see). Include only the basic body parts, such as stomach, muscles, heart, and blood.

2. On a large sheet of paper, draw an outline of a man and woman, leaving out all the details. What parts would they add for the picture for it to be a man? To be a woman? Have group members draw in the parts adding as many details as they can, including genitals and body hair. Review the location and function

of sexual body parts. Review the fact that each of us is either a male or female and that is determined by certain sexual body parts.

3. Female Body Parts

• Using the female adult drawing in the Assessment section, have the group members identify the sexual parts for the female in the following ways: (1) pointing to the part after the group leader names it, or (2) naming the part after the group leader points to it. Identify breast area, pubic area, and vulva. Talk about internal parts including the uterus, ovaries, and egg (ovum). Also discuss urinary opening, anus, and vagina, which are the three openings in the woman's "bottom" or "crotch" area. These openings and the buttocks are other areas that are considered private areas (see Goal #4: Understanding Public and Private Behavior, in this section, for activities on private/public).

• In simple, understandable terms, explain the function of the female sexual parts. For example, you might say that the female has two ovaries, one on each side low in the abdomen (or belly). The ovaries store the female sex cells called "eggs" or "ova." Be careful to clarify that these eggs are not the size of chicken eggs that we cook and eat, but that they are very tiny, the size of a pin head. Have the youths tell you their understanding of the function of the sexual parts. (See Goal #7: Understanding Sexual Feelings and Behaviors, and Goal #8: Understanding Reproduction, in this section, and include them in the discussion of intercourse and conception.) Group members can also locate and describe the function of other female body parts such as the clitoris and fallopian tubes.

4. Male Body Parts

• Using a drawing of an adult male (see the the Assessment section for the illustration), have group members identify the sexual parts for male in the following ways: (1) pointing to the part after the group leader names it, (2) naming the part after the group leader points to it. At a minimum, include the penis, testicles and pubic area. Include the anus in the discussion, as it is a private body part on the male.

- In simple, understandable words, explain the function of the male sexual parts. For example: Sperm is the male sex cell, which is produced by the testicles. It is so tiny, you can't see it without a microscope.

- Have the students tell you the function of the sexual parts you have discussed to check their understanding. (See Goal #7: Understanding Sexual Feelings and Behaviors, and Goal #8: Understanding Reproduction, in this section, and include them in the discussion of intercourse and conception.) Other specific male body sexual parts may also be discussed with group members who may be able to understand more detail, including parts of the penis (glans and shaft), scrotum, sperm ducts, and so on.

5. Have group members list the slang words for each sexual part. Give the anatomical name for each part and discuss the reasons for knowing these terms.

6. Discuss that everyone's body looks different from others', including their sexual parts. Just as hair- and eye-color differ, so do body-height and weight, and the size and shape of sexual body parts. For example, talk about the fact that some women have small breasts and some women have large breasts; some men have a small penis and some men have a large penis. Even though we are all different, we are still "okay."

7. The slide program, *Life Horizons I*, by Winifred Kempton, (see the Resources section) is useful for teaching sexual awareness. The teacher can individualize the information presented with the slides for the individual learners.

GOAL 4:   Understanding Public and Private Behavior

Activities

1. Review the concepts of privacy and private.

- Privacy is when no one else is around.

- We all have the right to be alone (to be private) at times.

- Your body has private parts.

- Some activities, such as using the toilet, are private and need to be done in private places, usually when no one else is around.

- We need to respect others' need for privacy.

2. Help group members identify their "private" places; for example, at home (bedroom, bathroom), or at school or work (locker, desk, bathroom). Talk about the importance of each person respecting the privacy of others.

3. Discuss what parts of the body are considered "private." Talk about sexual and other related parts, including genital areas, breasts, and buttocks. Using drawings of a male and female (see the Assessment section for illustrations), have the group members identify the private parts of the body. Drawing or pasting a picture of a bathing suit or underwear can identify private parts. Anatomically correct dolls are useful for demonstrating this concept.

4. Talk about rules for touching of private parts. Review with group members that in most cases, no one should touch another person unless he/she wants to be touched, on either their public or private parts. Discuss that there are certain times when it is okay for certain people to touch your private parts—like when a parent, nurse, physician, or other caregiver may need to touch a private part (if you are sick or hurt), or, if you feel that you are old enough and mature enough to be sexual with another person and both of you agree that the touching of private parts is okay.

5. Discuss "private" activities and behavior—things that we do in private places, when other people are not around. Identify activities which are done in private places, including bathing, taking a shower, using the toilet, undressing/dressing, touching your own sexual parts for pleasure (masturbation), and sexual behavior (kissing, "necking," "petting," and intercourse).

6. Introduce the concept of "public"—that is, when other people are around.

7. Help group members identify "public" places, for example: at home (kitchen, living room, or yard), at school or work (classroom, office) or in the community (store, bus stop). Combine with Activity #2 above, in the current group of activities.

8. Discuss what parts of the body are considered "public." Use drawings of a male and female (see the Assessment section for illustrations) to point out the "public" parts—or the parts of the body that it is okay for other people to see. Anatomically correct dolls are also useful for demonstrating this concept. Combine with Activity #3 (private body parts) above, in the current group of activities. Remind group members that even if a part is a public part, that "you don't have to be touched on the public part if you don't want to be."

9. Discuss "public" activities or behavior. These include those things that are okay to do in front of other people. Combine this discussion with Activity #5 (public body parts) above, in the current group of activities.

10. Meet individual needs of group members in regards to private/public.

   - You may need to discuss the fact that some participants need help with bathing and toileting. This might require the caregiver to touch private parts in order to assist with toileting or bathing, activities that are considered private, occurring in a private place. Discuss with the participant individually as needed.

   - For some participants to learn socially acceptable behavior, it may be necessary to give individualized instruction with specific rules about "private" and "public" behavior and places. For example, it may be okay to touch themselves, or masturbate, in the shower or the bathroom in their home (which are "private" places), but it would not be okay to masturbate in the bathroom or shower while at school or work (these are more like "public" places).

   - As a trainer, think about how you would respond if a person engaged in a "private" activity (e.g., masturbation) in a non-private or public place. It is usually best to interrupt the behavior and give information about if, when, and where the behavior is okay. Then redirect to another activity. Try to teach rather than scold.

GOAL 5: Differentiating Between Inappropriate and Appropriate Touching

Activities

1. Review concept of "private" and "public" body parts, behavior and activities. (See Goal #4: Understanding Public and Private Behavior, in this section.) Also talk about people who may and who may not be allowed to touch private parts. (Doctors, nurses, attendants, parents, boyfriends, girlfriends, husbands, and wives are sometimes allowed to touch the private parts of our bodies.)

2. Help group members identify types of touches. Talk about:

    *   "Good" touch—a nurturing touch that feels like something is being given or shared; such as a hug, holding hands with a friend or a family member, having your sister brush your hair, or a back rub. Think about how nice these things feel.

    *   "Bad" touch—a touch that is painful or feels like something is being taken away; as when someone hits or kicks you, a mosquito bites you or a bee stings you, or bruising your knee when you fall down. Think about how bad or "yucky" these things feel. A "bad" touch might also be when someone touches you in a private place (as in sexual abuse) or in a way that feels bad or in any way that you don't want.

    *   "Confusing" touch—any touch that cannot be clearly labeled as bad or good. Any touch may become "confusing" when (1) the meaning of the touch is not clear, (2) the person doing the touching doesn't usually behave in this way, or (3) the touching becomes sexual and the receiver is confused about it. For example, sometimes things in the "good" touch list don't feel good—like getting hugged by a relative when you don't want to be hugged. Another example is when someone you like, and who is usually nice to you, touches you in a way that feels uncomfortable—tickling too long, or touching you in a private place.

3. Discuss inappropriate touching. Use examples of situations that include varying aspects of people and places. For example, "Is it okay to touch your brother's penis?" "Is it okay to touch your own penis or vulva when you are in a public place?"

S.T.A.R.S. © 2008 by Susan Heighway and Susan Kidd Webster. Future Horizons, Inc.

In the section on Assertiveness, there are activities for learning how to avoid or respond to unwanted touches.

GOAL 6:   Understanding the Emotional and Physical Changes of Puberty

This STARS guidebook is designed for older adolescents and adults. Many of the individuals for whom this book is intended will have gone through puberty already. However, a review of the changes during puberty may be helpful for group members who would like a review, or who have not learned about their bodies and puberty.

Activities

1. Ask participants to bring photographs of themselves at different ages. Discuss how their bodies have changed from birth. If photographs aren't available, cut pictures out of magazines of people at different stages of development.

2. *Life Horizons I*, Part 2: Sexual Life Cycle, by Winifred Kempton (see the Resources section for reference) may be useful for reviewing body changes for both men and women.

3. Explain puberty using simple terms and understandable ideas. For example, your explanation might include that, at a certain point or time period in your life, usually when you were around ten or eleven years old, your body knew that it was time to change to become a grown-up. This time is called puberty and your body began to change to look more like grown-ups' bodies. Changes take place both inside and outside the body. Some are obvious, but others occur inside the body, where we cannot see them. Have group members tell you about puberty to review their understanding.

4. Review specific body changes that happened during puberty. Identify specific characteristics that make grown-ups look different from children—they are taller, and may have body hair, breasts, or big muscles.

- In girls, the changes that appear in puberty include breasts starting to enlarge, pubic hair appearing, hair appearing under the arms, growing taller, and beginning menstruation.

- In boys, the changes that appear in puberty include testes and penis getting bigger, pubic hair appearing, voice changing, ejaculation becoming possible and/or more frequent, growing taller, hair appearing under arms and on legs and chest, and beard developing.

5. Explain that during puberty, young women begin to experience sexual changes. Most girls begin to experience an increase in sexual feelings in addition to body changes, which gradually lessen, as the female grows older. Having sexual dreams and fantasies and becoming sexually excited is a normal part of growing up. Emphasize in the discussion that just because a young woman has become aware of sexual feelings or sexual arousal, it is not necessary to act on those feelings with others (be explicit when explaining intimate behavior with others).

6. Explain menstruation, or having a period. Use simple and understandable words. There is a wide spectrum of need for information among women with cognitive limitations, and it is important to consider what amount is needed for each woman. Consider whether the woman needs just enough information to understand that menstruation is normal for adult women, and whether more information would be too abstract and confusing for her. Or does the woman need much more information because she has higher cognitive capabilities and is capable of understanding that a female can become pregnant after she has begun menstruating?

   - Explain that menstruation happens to girls only. It begins during puberty when a girl's body is developing and she is becoming a woman. It is a natural process and it will happen until a woman is in her forties or fifties. It is also called a period.

   - Use pictures or an anatomically correct doll to show as explicitly as possible where the menstrual blood flows. Ask the group members to tell you about menstruation to check their understanding, including slang words.

   - Point out (to those women who will understand) that when a girl is mature enough to menstruate, her body has gone through changes that make it

S.T.A.R.S. © 2008 by Susan Heighway and Susan Kidd Webster. Future Horizons, Inc.

possible for her to become pregnant. (See Goal #7: Understanding Sexual Feelings and Behaviors, the next goal in this section, for activities regarding intercourse and pregnancy.)

- Review use of feminine hygiene products. Women may appreciate the opportunity to view the products without men present. Find out if any group members need specific training about menstrual management and arrange to provide that training yourself or ask a significant other to assist with the training.

- Young men will also benefit from basic information about menstruation. It can help them to better understand the female body, what girls are going through, and to clarify any misinformation. Provide the opportunity for young men to view feminine hygiene products and give a brief explanation. Some of the more explicit discussion about the use of feminine hygiene products by women may be more appropriate for women only.

- Discuss other concerns about menstruation including cramps, recording menstrual cycles, managing PMS, and minor uncomfortable symptoms.

7. Explain that during puberty, boys experience sexual changes. Most young men will experience a normal increase in sexual feelings, causing more frequent erections of their penis, which is normal. Having sexual dreams and fantasies and becoming sexually excited is a normal part of growing up. Emphasize, though, that it is not necessary to act on sexual feelings (be explicit about intimate behavior with others) just because the youth becomes aware of these feelings.

8. Explain an erection using simple understandable terms. Figure out how much detail to use based on the understanding capabilities of the men. Show tasteful (not pornographic) pictures of males to compare the penis in a flaccid state and in an erect state. Discuss the slang words for erection.

- Explain that erection is when the penis gets stiff and hard when a boy/man is sexually excited. It can happen often when a boy is going through puberty, sometimes from seeing a sexually attractive person or from physical stimulation from clothing or touching. It happens less often as males mature. Remind the men that if an erection happens when they are in a public place, it is not okay to touch their penis. Sometimes ejaculation occurs with an erection. (See the next activity, Activity #9, for an explanation of ejaculation.)

- Females also benefit from basic information about male functions. It will help them to better understand the male body, what men experience, and to clarify any misinformation. If presenting information in a group setting, it will depend on the comfort level.

- Discuss erection in more detail, linking erection with intercourse, for men who will understand. To explain, you might say that males are built the way they are and have erections of their penis because that is part of the process of creating babies. A male's penis is designed to be able to fit inside a woman's vagina, and it needs to be erect to do that. Check the understanding of the men by asking them to tell you about erection.

9. Explain ejaculation. Use simple, understandable terms. To explain, you might say that when older boys and men are sexually excited the penis has an erection. If the penis is stimulated enough, the male will have an orgasm, which is a very strong and good feeling in the area around the penis. At the time of the orgasm, a thick white fluid, called semen, which carries sperm, comes out quickly from the end of the penis (about a tablespoonful). Check the understanding of the men by asking them to explain ejaculation. Identify slang words for ejaculation.

GOAL 7: Understanding Sexual Feelings and Behaviors

Activities

1. Review romantic relationships. For activities, see Goal #4: Engaging in More Mature Relationships, in the Social Interaction section.

2. Discuss behaviors that are considered sexual, as well as the range of sexual behaviors that can be associated with a romantic relationship. Also consider values and social rules that are related to sexual expression. (For related activities, see Goal #9: Examining Societal Norms and Values Regarding Sexuality, in this section.)

List behaviors that two people in a romantic relationship might engage in to express their affection for each other. Include giving compliments and gifts, holding hands, hugging, kissing, "necking," "petting," and having intercourse. Clarify what the terms mean. For example, "necking" or "making out" means having prolonged kissing sessions. Help group members understand which behaviors are acceptable in romantic relationships, but not acceptable in other relationships.

3. Discuss sexual orientation. Some people have or want a sexual partner of the opposite sex to care about and to have sexual relations with—this sexual orientation is called heterosexual. Other people have or want a sexual partner of the same sex to care about and have a sexual relationship with—this sexual orientation is called homosexual. Use the correct terminology: a female homosexual is also called a lesbian; a male can be called gay or a homosexual. (For more discussion activities, see Goal #9: Examining Societal Norms and Values Regarding Sexuality, in this section.)

4. Explain masturbation. You might say that masturbation is when a person, either male or female, touches their own sexual parts (private parts or genitals) by stroking or rubbing them, which feels very good and is sexually stimulating. Use an illustration (see the illustrations in the Assessment section). Emphasize that masturbation is done in a private place and identify these possible places with the group members. (See Activity #4 in Goal #4: Understanding Public and Private Behavior, in this section, to combine this with a discussion of private and public behavior. See Activity #1 in Goal #9: Examining Societal Norms and Values Regarding Sexuality, in this section, to combine this discussion with values about sexual behavior.)

5. Explain orgasm. Orgasm happens in women and in men. Explain that when a person (male or female) is sexually excited, sometimes he/she experiences a build-up of sexual (erotic) tension. The heart might beat faster and stronger, there is more rapid breathing, and muscular may get tense. This tension increases to a certain level until there is a release, which is often sudden. After the release, there is usually a feeling of well being, relaxation, or relief. Some educators have likened an orgasm to the sensations that occur in a sneeze—a beginning tickle, a build up of tension, and then a sudden release with a feeling of relief.

6. Explain intercourse. First review male and female sexual body parts, including the penis and the vulva/vagina, and review erection. Your explanation needs to be simple and understandable. You might say: "When a grown man and a grown woman love each other in a sexual way, they may want to have intercourse. While they are in a private place, kissing, hugging, and touching each other on their bodies usually sexually excites both the man and the woman, including their private parts. When a man gets sexually excited, his penis will become erect, and when a woman gets excited, her vagina/vulva may become moist from secretions. Intercourse is when the man puts his erect penis into the woman's vagina. Moving back and forth can feel very good for both the man and the woman and usually causes orgasms to occur for both the man (he will usually ejaculate sperm) and the woman. This is the way a woman can become pregnant."

    Combine this discussion of intercourse with the content on the prevention of pregnancy (abstinence and contraception). For activities, see Goal #8: Understanding Reproduction in Sexual Awareness, below. Also emphasize the benefits of a monogamous relationship.

GOAL 8:   Understanding Reproduction

Activities

1. Explain fertilization. Review internal and external sexual body parts using activities from Goal #3: Identifying Body Parts and Understanding Their Functions, in this section, and review sexual activity and intercourse using activities from Goal #7: Understanding Sexual Feelings and Behaviors, in this section.

    *   Explain by saying that fertilization happens during or after intercourse. If it is the time of the month when a woman's ovary has produced an egg (an ovum), the act of intercourse could result in fertilization and a pregnancy. This occurs when sperm meet up with the egg in the woman's body and the egg is fertilized and attaches to the uterus wall.

    *   In your discussion be clear about the size of the egg—that it is very tiny, not like a chicken egg. Do not use terminology like "planting a seed," as some books suggest. People with cognitive disabilities usually think very concretely and they could take this very literally, meaning that they "plant

a seed, such as an apple seed or a watermelon seed, in their vagina if they want to have a baby.

• Help participants understand that pregnancy is a result of intercourse, and check for understanding.

2. Discuss pregnancy. Explain that pregnancy happens only after a man and a woman have had intercourse and fertilization occurs. The fertilized ovum, which attaches to the uterine wall, starts growing there. Pregnancy normally lasts nine months. After about four months, the mother's abdomen begins to get noticeably larger as the baby grows inside the uterus. Clarify that the baby does not grow in the stomach (where our food goes), but in the uterus. Check group members' understanding by having them describe pregnancy, using pictures or anatomically correct dolls.

Other areas of discussion might include: How does a woman know when she is pregnant? Talk about having intercourse, missing a period, noticing some physical changes, and going to the doctor for a pregnancy test. Talk about the placenta and umbilical cord. Discuss multiple births.

3. Explain labor and delivery. Explain labor and the birthing process to help group members understand how the baby gets out of the mother's body. A birth of a baby usually occurs in the hospital where doctors and nurses can help. Talk about both types of births, vaginal delivery and Cesarean section (C-section). Pictures or anatomical models that show the woman's whole body during delivery are helpful. (Sometimes these can be borrowed from public schools or agencies that sponsor birthing classes.) Talk about the labor and birth as being a lot of work. Many women talk about it as being painful, but worth it.

4. Discuss the prevention of pregnancy by abstaining from intercourse (which means not having intercourse, the only absolutely sure way to prevent pregnancy). Assure group members that it is okay to have sexual feelings, but sexual intercourse does not have to be the only way to express those feelings. If a person decides not to have sexual intercourse, identify ways to avoid situations where intercourse can easily happen. For example, discuss with group members that, to avoid intercourse, "you could choose social activities in a group instead of doing something alone with your intimate partner. It may be hard to stop

sexual activity if you and your partner are in a private place and get sexually excited." Remind group members that each person can make their own decision without necessarily worrying about pleasing their partner, or giving in to peer pressure.

5. Discuss the prevention of pregnancy by using contraception, or birth control. To promote understanding for group members, a discussion of contraception should follow a review of intercourse and the process of fertilization. (For activities, see Activity #6 in Goal #7: Understanding Sexual Feelings and Behaviors, and Activity #1 in Goal #8: Understanding Reproduction, in this section.)

- You might explain that when a man and woman are very much in love and want to show their love through intercourse, but they do not want to have a baby, they can prevent pregnancy through birth control or contraception. Birth control stops the sperm and egg from coming together to produce a fertilized egg, which grows into a baby.

- Assess each participant's need for information about birth control. Not all group members need to have detailed information. Generally, if a person can understand intercourse, then he/she can likely understand the concept of birth control. The most essential information to provide about birth control includes (1) why it is used, (2) when to use it, (3) that there are different types of methods, and (4) who can help the person to obtain birth control.

  Presenting many specific types of birth control measures at one time may be confusing for the person, especially for a person with a cognitive disability. Instead, arrange for a one-to-one conversation with the person to provide direction about the best type of birth control for his/her abilities and situation.

- Assist group members in identifying helpful adults with whom to discuss birth control—perhaps a physician, nurse practitioner, or a professional at a family planning clinic in the community. Talk about how to ask for information and support about birth control.

- Provide specific instruction on birth control methods as indicated. For example, providing information about using condoms is helpful for many reasons. Explain that condoms are mentioned widely on the radio, on TV, and in magazines as being useful in the prevention of pregnancy, and in the prevention of the spread of HIV and other sexually transmitted diseases. Condoms are readily available in stores and many people have heard of them.

- Provide explicit information about condom use, that is, knowing exactly when and how to use a condom. Demonstrate use of a condom using a life-size model of a penis. Be sure to explain step-by-step specifics of condom use: once the penis is erect, and before intercourse, put the condom on by placing it on the tip of the penis and gently unrolling it and so on. Other essential information to include: Latex condoms are safest. Condoms in wrappers are safe for six months. After that, discard them to avoid the chance of them breaking or tearing by accident. Condoms work best with non-oxynyl-9, a jelly-like substance that coats the condom and acts as a spermicide.

6. Explain sterilization. This means methods of birth control that are permanent. Sterilization is suitable for only those men and women who have decided never to cause conception or become pregnant. (There are laws about who can be sterilized. See the Resources section for references.)

7. Explain abortion. Explain that abortion is a surgical procedure done by a licensed physician (medical doctor) to end a pregnancy, usually within the first one to four months of pregnancy. Abortion is a serious procedure to remove the fetus and placenta and a doctor does this in a medical clinic or a hospital. A person must never perform an abortion on herself. Abortion should not be substituted for the use of other birth control measures. Abortion is legal in the United States, but people have differing views on whether abortion is ethical or moral.

GOAL 9: Examining Societal Norms and Values Regarding Sexuality

Activities

1. Begin a group/individual discussion to explore beliefs about the rules of society that govern sexual behavior. Create a list of different sexual activities, which

might include hugging, kissing, sexual touching with a partner, masturbation, and sexual intercourse.

Present the concept of values and social rules as guidelines that we go by in order to know how to act in an acceptable way. For example, what rules are there in your home, or in your workplace? Each type of setting where group members live, work, and hang out will have its own rules and expectations regarding sexual activity. Individuals in the group may be living in a variety of settings. These settings could include their own home, a family member's home, a group home, or a supported apartment. Group members may be working or spending their days in a variety of vocational, educational, or recreational settings as well. For each of the activities list values/social rules for them. Discuss these rules with participants and how their lives are affected by them. For example, discuss:

- When is it okay to hug someone?

- How well should you know someone before you touch each other in a sexual way?

- When is it okay to have sexual intercourse? You might start the discussion with, "Some people have strong feelings about sexual intercourse, such as the belief that it is only okay if the man and woman are married. Other people have different values/ideas and feel that if two people care about each other very much and they want to express their love with sexual intercourse, it is okay even if they are not married. What do you think?"

- Masturbation is another value-laden behavior. Your discussion may include the following points: "Is it okay to masturbate? When and where? People have different ideas about masturbation—some people think that it is terrible and wrong and should never be done. Other people think it is normal and healthy and that it is okay in a private place. What do you think?"

- Homosexuality. Many people believe that homosexuality is an acceptable sexual orientation, that it is okay for men to desire men for sexual partners (terms for this sexual orientation are "gay" or "homosexual") and for women to desire women as sexual partners (terms for this sexual orientation are "lesbian" or "homosexual"). Other people do not accept homosexuality as

S.T.A.R.S. © 2008 by Susan Heighway and Susan Kidd Webster. Future Horizons, Inc.

a sexual orientation. They have strong ideas about which sex an intimate sexual partner should be, that men should only desire woman for sexual partners and that women should only desire men for sexual partners. There are slang terms which are rude to use, including "fag," "dyke," or "homo." Remind group members that these are hurtful terms no matter what a person's belief and it is not okay to use them.

2. Present the concept of mutual consent in sexual behavior. Mutual consent means that two people both agree that the sexual behavior between them is okay, whether it is touching, hugging, kissing, or intercourse. Otherwise, if either one of the people does not agree to the behavior, it is never okay to do these behaviors. Talk about sexual assault and include the full spectrum of assault, from unwanted sexual touching to rape. (See the section on Assertiveness for specifics on personal safety.)

3. Address decision-making regarding sexual situations. This discussion makes the most sense when an individual is dating or thinking about a romantic relationship.

Discuss some important things to think about when making decisions about showing sexual feelings. Some people prefer abstinence, which is the choice to not have sexual intercourse at all until in you are in a committed relationship or are married. To do this, individuals often need information and support. This section may be useful in helping participants who are in serious romantic relationships to consider their options and their behavior. Following are some important discussion points.

- Ask the person: Do you feel you're ready? Do you feel you can be responsible for your actions, which affect you and another person?

- Advise the person: Be sure the other person feels just as you do. Never force anyone into anything.

- Guide the person to a supportive adult: If you can, discuss these issues with an adult that you trust, perhaps your parent, guardian, support worker, or friend. Who is a safe and supportive adult for you?

- Advise: Think about sexual behavior ahead of time, that is, before being in a situation that necessitates decision-making.

- Discuss how a person might know that he/she is ready for a sexual relationship. To be ready to engage in sexual behavior, it is best if a person has the ability to:

  » Understand that the enjoyment of sexuality involves the ability to make thoughtful decisions.

  » Talk comfortably with their partner about preventing unintended pregnancy and STDs.

  » Understand whether they are exploiting another person or being exploited.

  » Make the emotional commitment and take on the obligation of a healthy adult sexual relationship.

4. Use a story to discuss decision-making. Sometimes it is easier for group members to use a story about someone else when thinking about sensitive situations related to sexuality. Use pictures in books or magazines and develop a story for the participants to relate to. Develop stories to illustrate some of the relationship issues that group members may be experiencing. For example, the following story makes the point that there are other ways to express feelings and to be with your intimate sexual partner than to just have sex.

"Suppose that Kim and Eric care about each other very much and have very strong emotional feelings for each other. They both have decided they are not ready for sexual intercourse, but they do want to share their sexual feelings. What are ways they can show their affection?" (To review sexual behaviors in romantic relationships, see Goal #7: Understanding Sexual Feelings and Behaviors, in this section.) "How can they figure out what they will do?" (Answers may include: talk to each other, talk to a trusted adult to get advice and suggestions.)

Present other brief situations and ask group members for their opinions about what they would do. You can list two or three alternatives for each situation, and then discuss what might be the consequences of each decision.

GOAL 10: Learning about Sexually Transmitted Diseases

Activities

1. To help group members grasp the concept of sexually transmitted diseases, it is helpful to talk about how other common diseases are spread. Review how people get common diseases; most are spread from person to person. For example, the common cold is spread from germs, which can be passed by sneezing into air that is breathed in by another person, or if someone sneezes on their hands and then touches another person.

2. "STDs" or sexually transmitted diseases (in the past these were called venereal diseases) are diseases that can be spread by germs through having sexual contact with someone who has the disease. The only way to "catch" a STD is through sexual contact with someone who already has the disease. Be explicit about describing the sexual contact (e.g., vagina and penis; vagina and mouth; penis and anus). Anatomically correct dolls are useful for this.

3. Review some of the names of the diseases, identifying both the slang words and the medical terminology: human papilloma virus (HPV), gonorrhea, herpes, chlamydia, syphilis, and HIV infection.

4. Other important points about STDs:

   - If you have not had sexual contact, you don't need to worry about having caught a STD.

   - If you are thinking about having sexual contact with a partner, consider what to do about preventing the spread of STDs such as:

     » Asking your partner if he/she has a disease of the sexual parts.

     » Using "safer sex" practices, such as using a condom or having no sexual contact.

» If you find out your sex partner has a sexually transmitted disease and you have had sexual contact, and even if you don't have symptoms, you should go to your doctor for a check-up.

5. Review the symptoms that may indicate that a person has an illness or a problem that needs to be checked by a doctor or nurse practitioner, including unusual discharge from the penis or vagina, sores, rashes, itching, blisters, or pain around the genitals. Sometimes these symptoms are due to STDs and sometimes they are due to other causes, such as a urinary tract infection, and not an STD.

6. You may want to discuss HIV infection specifically. Include in the discussion:

- The serious nature of the HIV infection, the course of the disease, treatment.

- Routes of transmission and risk behaviors. People can get infected with HIV from blood to blood contact (this includes blood transfusions, sharing needles when using injectable illicit drugs) or sexual contact (multiple partners, not using safer sex practices).

- Emphasize the importance of being able to talk to your sexual partner. This means that you have to know them well enough so that you know their sexual habits and whether you can trust them to be honest about being infected or not, and to use safer sex practices (condom or abstinence).

- Present correct information and dispel misconceptions, such as the myth that HIV infection can be "caught" by just shaking hands with a person who has HIV infection. For more specific information on teaching about HIV infection, refer to the Resources section for references. You may want to invite a guest speaker from the local Public Health Department or other agency who is knowledgable about STDs. It is important that the speaker is able to present the information at a level that the participants will find comprehendable and useful.

GOAL 11: Discussing Other Health Issues Related to Sexual Awareness

Activities

1. Review the importance of keeping the whole body clean. As an adult, there is a need for deodorant and possibly more frequent bathing, showering, and washing.

2. You might also want to discuss the importance of behaviors that promote health, including eating nutritious foods, getting enough sleep, and exercising.

3. Discuss the effect that using drugs and alcohol can have on judgment, especially about sexual behavior. A person who is under the influence of alcohol or drugs is more likely to lack judgment about engaging in sexual intercourse, to find themselves in dangerous situations such as being exposed to sexually transmitted diseases, or to be a victim of sexual assault.

4. Discuss the pressures from peers to use drugs and alcohol and how this may affect judgment in sexual behavior.

Community or Informal Activities

1. Look for opportunities in daily life to reinforce learning and answer questions related to sexuality. Seize the "teachable moment."

2. It may be necessary to assist individuals in preparing for and participating in physical (including gynecological) exams. Find sensitive health care providers who will offer support to the person and and help increase the person's awareness and comfort with sexuality.

section six

Assertiveness

Increasing Self-Empowerment through Words and Actions

Recognizing a Situation as Potentially Unsafe

Learning to Say "No" and Using Basic Self-Protection

Knowing How and Where to Get Help at Home and in the Community

Reporting Sexual Exploitation or Abuse

Assertiveness

Assertiveness is highly valued in our society. Learning to communicate and behave in ways that preserve our dignity and individuality and protect our personal interests is something we all seek and value. When people with developmental disabilities develop skills to express their needs, desires, choices, and opinions, they can then protect themselves from exploitative or abusive relationships, and also develop and sustain healthy relationships. The behaviors involved in meeting new people, inviting someone to a social event, and accepting or turning down a social invitation all require assertiveness.

Being assertive is especially difficult for people who have been taught to be dependent, to be passive and compliant, and to trust others' opinions about what is best for them. But it is best for everyone to foster choice-making and create opportunities for the person to make real choices in both small and important areas of his/her life.

While assertiveness training should include "stranger danger" concepts, the focus should clearly be on learning to be assertive with people with whom the participants have ongoing relationships or contact. We know that 90% of sexual abuse of people with developmental disabilities is perpetrated by someone the victim knows. It is crucial to help participants assert themselves with their friends, family, and support providers. For individuals who are not able to learn assertiveness behaviors and who are highly vulnerable (e.g., people who have profound mental retardation), the family and support providers need to develop a safety net that assures a safe environment.

Research tells us that victims of sexual abuse are frequently chosen not because of their sexual attractiveness, but because of their perceived powerlessness and non-assertive demeanor. People with developmental disabilities are frequently viewed as easy targets by perpetrators. Sex offenders often assume that these persons will not understand what is happening to them, and that they will neither be able to defend themselves against assault, nor be able to tell others about the incident. To counter these assumptions, personal empowerment needs to be an essential part of any program aimed at the prevention of abuse.

> "Perpetrators pick people who are less powerful than they are. Sexual assault is an abuse of power and relationships between people."
>
> —Sex therapist

> "Projecting an assertive image discourages abuse. Once protective behaviors have been learned, it becomes part of daily life—in work, in social relationships, and in the family."
>
> —Rape crisis worker

GOAL 1:   Increasing Self-Empowerment through Words and Actions

Activities

1. Group sharing. Have participants take turns telling the group about something good that happened to them that week. Focus on the successes individuals experienced that week, problems they solved, or situations they feel they handled well.

2. Group discussion. What are some of the things in your life that you would like to change? What are you happy with and want to keep the same?

3. Group discussion. Talk about how we express our feelings and how we can let others know what we want or need. Have group members practice using words and actions that they can use to tell others what they need, want, or don't want.

4. Role-play. Practice situations in which the individual makes a choice and conveys that choice to another person. For example: You are in a store trying on a dress and the salesperson tells you it looks great and urges you to buy it. You don't like the way the dress looks, but feel pressured by the salesperson. Practice saying, "No, I don't like the way the dress looks. I'd like to try on a different dress."

GOAL 2:   Recognizing a Situation as Potentially Unsafe

Activities

1. Help group members identify dangers in their everyday lives. Danger is something that is not safe; it is something that could possibly hurt you. For example:

    •   Getting hit by a car on a street with lots of traffic

    •   Going into deep water if you don't know how to swim

- Using the stove to cook some food if you don't how to

2. Discuss the meaning of personal safety, including:

- Keeping yourself safe

- Recognizing when you feel unsafe

- Knowing how to protect yourself

- Being able to enjoy going out alone or with friends.

3. Begin a group discussion about feeling safe or unsafe. Discuss times when you knew you were safe. What did that feel like? Talk about times when you felt unsafe, frightened or embarrassed and what caused these feelings. Have group members complete sentences such as, "When I'm alone at home I feel ..."

4. Review content on "strangers." (See Activities #7 through #9 in Goal #2: Identifying Persons in One's Life, in the Understanding Relationships section.) Review that a stranger is any person you do not know; if you don't know their name, then they are a stranger. Some strangers are community helpers and citizens like doctors, nurses, police officers, or adults with children. Most strangers are not dangerous. Other strangers may be dangerous strangers or someone who might hurt you. Dangerous strangers might be hard to pick out just by looking at them, so always trust your "gut feelings." (See Activity #6 in Goal #2: Recognizing A Situation as Potentially Unsafe, in this section, for reviewing the concept of "gut feelings.")

5. Review with participants the concepts of good, bad, and confusing touches. (See Activity #2 in Goal #5: Differentiating Between Inappropriate and Appropriate Touching, in this section.) Talk about good touches that feel nice—for example, a hug from your good friend when you want one. Bad touches feel bad—for example, a kick in the leg that hurts. A confusing touch is a touch that isn't clearly good or bad—for example, when someone you like and who is usually nice to you touches you in a way that doesn't feel right.

6. Review the concept of trusting your own "gut feelings." (See Activity #10 in Goal #2: Identifying Persons in One's Life, in the Understanding Relationships

section.) Talk about how you feel when you are scared—your heart pounds, you breathe quickly, and your hands sweat. This means your body is responding to something that isn't quite right. Sometimes, you may feel these "scared" feelings when you are around a stranger. You might also feel these "scared" feelings when you're around someone you know. Pay attention to the way you feel inside and the way your body feels outside; be in touch with your feelings.

7. Discuss sexual abuse. Begin by reviewing sexual body parts (see Goal #3: Identifying Body Parts and Understanding Their Functions, in this section) and appropriate and inappropriate touching (see Goal #5: Differentiating Between Inappropriate and Appropriate Touching, in this section). Anatomically correct dolls can be helpful here. Be careful to end this discussion on a positive note—that there are ways to protect yourself from sexual abuse.

   • Define sexual abuse, also called sexual assault. Sexual abuse is when someone engages in sexual activity with another person (e.g., touching the private parts, or having intercourse) without their permission or against their will. This would feel like a "bad" or "confusing" touch. Sexual abuse is also when anyone shows their private parts to another person or asks the other person to touch their private parts for sexual excitement without their permission or against their will. The person doing the sexual abuse could be a familiar person or a stranger.

   • Talk about rape. Carefully explain what it means. Rape usually means vaginal or anal intercourse without the person's permission or against their will.

   • Where can sexual abuse happen? It can happen almost anywhere, so it is important to learn how to identify whether or not you are safe, and learn how to protect yourself from the dangers.

   • Sexual abuse can happen to anyone—male or female, old or young.

   • Who is the perpetrator of sexual abuse? Who does it? Sexual abuse can happen with a stranger or someone who is familiar to the person. Usually we think of "dangerous" strangers as the people who do the sexual abuse—and we certainly must be careful of these people. Very often, though, sexual

S.T.A.R.S. © 2008 by Susan Heighway and Susan Kidd Webster. Future Horizons, Inc.

abuse takes place with someone the person knows. You cannot tell if a person is safe or not by how they look.

- You need to trust your "gut feelings." There are ways to protect yourself from sexual abuse.

GOAL 3: Learning to Say "No" and Using Basic Self-Protection

Activities

1. Review with group members the two main ways we express to others what we want, need, and feel: words (or "what we say"), and actions (or "what we do").

2. Group discussion. We have a right to say "no." No one should be touched unless he/she allows it. It is alright to say "no."

3. Role-plays. Help participants practice using words to say "no." Sometimes you say "no" gently, sometimes you say "no" very strongly.

   - Start with situations where participants can practice using the gentle "no," such as when one person has been invited to do something by another that the first doesn't want to do. For example: Your friend asks you to go bike riding. You are tired and don't want to go. Practice saying, "No, not today." Combine the role-play with group discussion about how it feels to say "no" to a friend.

   - Continue with situations to practice using the strong "no," where it seems one person is trying to hurt another person, or is trying to get the person to do something that he or she doesn't want to do. Responding with a strong "no" is necessary. For example: Two people are out on a date, and one person makes unwanted sexual advances, (which means trying to touch the person intimately, or on a private part). Practice saying a strong "no."

   - Help participants think of other strong statements, such as "leave me alone," "I don't want to," or "stop that." Talk about how this situation would feel, how to handle the situation if the unwanted behavior continues, and whether the group members would ever consider going on another date with the person.

4. Have group members practice saying "no" in various ways using actions, including facial expressions and body language. To get the idea, you might first show group members pictures of facial expressions such as "serious," "angry," or "firm," as well as pictures of body postures that express strong actions. Ask the group members if the pictures are saying "yes" or "no." Role-play situations in which participants use facial expressions and body language to indicate "no."

5. "What Would You Do?" Explain to group members that if they use words and actions together, the message will be even stronger. Give the students situations and help them to figure out, "What if that happened? What would I do or say?" Remember to practice using words and actions. You could do this activity by having individuals demonstrate their responses or having the group respond together. Use role-plays for the statements that are not sexual in nature. Following are some examples of "What Would You Do" questions.

    What would you do if:

    •   A stranger wants you to go for a walk with him or her?

    •   Your boss wanted to touch your private body parts?

    •   The bus driver says, "Come here next to me until everybody else gets off the bus"?

    •   Someone you know shows you his penis and asks you to touch it?

    •   Your job coach touches you in a way you don't like?

    •   Someone you know says, "I want to touch your penis (or vagina)"?

    •   Someone in an internet chat room asks you for your home address?

6. Discuss the effect of peer pressure on sexual activity. Young and older adults can be reassured that what they do with their own bodies is their business and nobody else's business. People with disabilities need to hear that they have the

freedom to make their own choices and that they are not abnormal if they want to delay sexual activity until they are ready. Help group members practice refusal skills for occasions when an individual might feel pressure to engage in sexual behavior before being ready, including statements such as "I like you and want to be friends with you, but I'm just not ready to have sex yet."

7. Discussion of home safety. At home there are rules you can follow to help keep you safe. Some group members will be capable of learning the rules and taking the responsibility for themselves, and others will require supervision because they have difficulty grasping the rules. Talk about and then role-play potentially dangerous situations. Allow individualized practice, depending on the needs of the group members. When doing the role-plays, provide situations that allow the students an opportunity to practice with "persistent" perpetrators. Prompt the participants with appropriate phrases. Remind role-players to use words and actions. Use of real props, such as a telephone, door, and doorbell, are best.

Answering the phone

- Say "Hello." If you decide to give the caller your name, use your first name only.

- Find out who is calling before giving any more information.

- Never say that you are home alone or that others are not there with you. If the person asks for someone who is not home, say, "They can't come to the phone right now," or "They are busy," or "He/she is in the shower." Ask if you can take a message or tell them to call back later.

- Never continue to talk with a stranger. Hang up if the person keeps asking more questions. If the phone call is obscene (the person starts using dirty language or saying nasty things), hang up.

Answering the door

- If you are home alone, never open the door unless you know the person well. Do you recognize the voice? Can you peek out a peephole or window to see them? If you are not positive about who is at the door, DO NOT open the door.

- Never say you are home alone. Just say something such as, "My roommate can't come to the door right now."

- Never give your name or phone number if the person asks for them. Just say, "I don't give out that information."

- Never leave your door unlocked if you are home alone. Lock the door (with a security chain, if you have one) and ground floor windows, too.

GOAL 4: Knowing How and Where to Get Help at Home and in the Community

Activities

1. Have participants list safe people in the community who could provide help when needed. Emphasize that police officers are often not immediately available when help is needed, so other safe people need to be identified, such as bus drivers, store clerks, neighbors, or job coaches.

2. Review the concept of "safe" strangers. (See Activity #9 in Goal 2: Identifying Persons in One's Life, in the Understanding Relationships section.)

3. Begin a group discussion about dealing with emergencies.

- Talk about: What is an emergency? Discuss fires, accidents, health problems, and robberies.

- What to do? Discuss with each group member—and their significant other—what the individual's plan is, according to the person's capabilities. Consider whether the person is capable of staying home alone, and what their capabilities are in the event that a caregiver or roommate is injured or needs help.

- Role-play. Practice getting help in various situations, such as using the telephone to call 911, or asking another person to help. For example: Would you call 911 if _____ ?

4. Discuss possible ways of getting help in an uncomfortable or dangerous situation. These situations might include times when someone is trying to hurt you, when there is a fire, or if you are with another person or caregiver and the person or caregiver has had an accident or injury and you need to get help. The ways of getting help may include:

- Making a noise or yelling to attract attention

- Walking or running to where there are other people

- Using a telephone to call for help.

GOAL 5: Reporting Sexual Exploitation or Abuse

Activities

1. Have each participant make a list of five people to go to for help. Examples include counselors, social workers, relatives, residential support workers, job coaches, and bosses. When identifying people, think about whether these people would listen to you. Do you think you could go to this person and tell them what happened?

- What should the person do if the first person they tell doesn't believe them or won't help them? Brainstorm ideas and potential helpers with the group.

- For each person, make cards that they can carry with them that have the names and phone numbers for these helpers.

2. Discuss how to report sexual abuse. You could role-play a situation like this, for example: A neighbor comes to your house and wants to borrow something. You are home alone and he asks you to touch a private part of his body. Practice saying "no." Practice talking to someone about it. Talk about what to do next if the first person they told did not believe them.

Community or Informal Activities

1. Make sure that participants carry phone numbers of people they can call for help.

2. Practice using pay phones.

3. Identify safe people in the community besides police officers who would usually be of assistance (store clerks, bus drivers).

4. Help participants locate nearby places to go if they need help, such as the police station, fire station, or hospital emergency room. This may help the individual become more comfortable should they need assistance.

5. If a person uses the internet, be sure to review internet safety tips and address issues such as:

   • Protecting identity

   • Meeting people online

   • Posting private information on message boards, blogs, and networking websites such as MySpace, Friendster, Facebook, etc.

   • Visiting websites with sexually explicit material.

See the Resources section for specific references.

Section seven

Assessment

STARS Participant Information Form

Sexual Attitudes and Knowledge (S.A.K.) Assessment

Sexual Abuse Risks Assessment (S.A.R.A.)

Individual Training Plan

STARS Participant Information Form

Date: _____

Source of Referral: _____

Participant's Name: _____

Address: _____

_____

Phone: _____

Date of Birth: _____

List primary service provider with contact persons and phone numbers
(e.g., residential, educational, vocational providers, or case manager):

_____

Guardianship status: _____

If the participant is not his/her own guardian, list the following information:

Guardian's Name: _____

Guardian's Address: _____

_____

_____

Guardian's Phone: _____

Assessment

We believe that it is important to assess the participant's knowledge and attitudes about sexuality and abuse prevention as well as to gather information about factors in their lives that may be increasing their risk for sexual abuse.

We have provided two assessment tools in this section for that purpose that include, the Sexual Attitudes and Knowledge (S.A.K.) Assessment and the Sexual Abuse Risk Assessment (S.A.R.A.). If you prefer, gathering the assessment information in a more informal manner is also appropriate. Reviewing the assessment tools may give you helpful suggestions for developing your individualized assessment.

THE SEXUAL ATTITUDES AND KNOWLEDGE (S.A.K.) ASSESSMENT

This tool can be used to evaluate the individual's attitudes, knowledge, and skills in the four content areas of STARS: Understanding Relationships, Social Interaction, Sexual Awareness, and Assertiveness.

The participant is asked by the trainer to respond to a series of questions, each accompanied by a picture (line drawing) that is included with the assessment. In developing this assessment tool, we found that adding the pictures as visual stimuli positively affected the participants' ability to respond to the questions.

We offer two versions of the S.A.K. assessment tool. The first and original version is the S.A.K. Question/Answer Form A: For Individuals with Ability to Answer Open-Ended Questions. The original worked with most individuals, yet we discovered people who seemed to understand the content, but were unable to answer open-ended questions. As a result, we adapted the original questions into yes/no questions and developed the S.A.K. Question/Answer Form B: For Individuals with Ability to Answer Yes/No Questions Only. When using this version, the individual must have the ability to indicate a clear yes/no answer.

The S.A.K. can be used:

- To identify learning needs of individuals to determine the specific goals and strategies for group training programs

- As a pre-training/post-training evaluation of a participant and to assess program effectiveness, or

- To design a one-to-one training program for an individual.

Using the S.A.K. Assessment Tool

It is best to administer the assessment on a one-to-one basis. Choose the appropriate version of the tool based on the abilities of the individual, either the S.A.K. Question/Answer Form A: For Individuals with Ability to Answer Open-Ended Questions, or the S.A.K. Question/Answer Form B: For Individuals with Ability to Answer Yes/No Questions Only.

Using the questions from the appropriate S.A.K. Question/Answer Form and the corresponding pictures for each, read each question to the participant. Read the questions as written. Use your own discretion in clarifying or simplifying the content as needed for the individual while preserving the essence of the question. When reading questions, avoid giving cues like facial expressions, gestures, or voice changes to direct the participant's answer. Mark the participant's answer in the proper blank on the Question/Answer Form.

We have found that some participants want to know whether or not they have answered correctly. The responses of the participants can be reviewed after each question/answer is completed or following completion of the entire tool.

Scoring

1. After the assessment is completed, refer to the Correct Answers for the version of the tool that you have used. Mark the number of points for each correct answer in the blank to the left of each question on the S.A.K. Question/Answer Form. All questions have point values for correct answers except for the attitude questions that are marked with an asterisk (*).

2. Use the Final Score Form for the version of the tool that you have used. Count the number of answers correct in each STARS content area. For each question, locate the number listed under the content areas. For example, find question #1, which is located under Understanding Relationships on the Final Score Form. Then transfer the score (# of correct points) from the Question/Answer Sheet to the proper blank.

3. For attitude questions, summarize the person's answers in the space under each category on the Final Score Form (except for the Assertiveness section, where there aren't any attitude questions).

Interpretation of Scores

1. Remember that this is just one type of measure of the individual's knowledge, skills, and attitudes. To get a full picture of their abilities, it is best to combine the information obtained from this assessment with other observations and experience with the individual.

2. Scores in each STARS content area can be used to assist the trainer in determining the individual's learning needs, strengths, and deficits in each area. For example, a score of 5 correct out of 6 points total in the Understanding Relationships section indicates that the individual probably has at least a beginning understanding of concepts for relationships presented in the assessment tool; whereas, a score of 6 correct out of 29 points in the Sexual Awareness section indicates that the individual probably has a knowledge deficit in this area. The summary of attitudes is used to better understand the attitudes of the individual, but not to make a judgment.

3. After scoring the assessment, the trainer can review the results to assist in:

   • Identifying concerns or knowledge deficits that may increase risks for sexual abuse, or that would interfere with the ability of the individual to develop a positive approach to sexuality or understanding of sexuality

   • Identifying strengths, positive aspects in the participant's attitudes, knowledge, and skills to build on.

This information, along with the results of the Sexual Abuse Risks Assessment (S.A.R.A.), which is also in this Assessment section of the STARS guidebook, will be helpful for developing an Individual Training Plan (see form at the end of this section).

S.A.K. QUESTION/ANSWER FORM A
For Individuals with Ability to Answer Open-Ended Questions

It is helpful to record responses to questions on a separate piece of paper for reference. After the questionnaire is completed, you can go back and check the participant's answers against the Correct Answers at the end of this form and record the points correct in the corresponding column. (Of course, if you are already familiar with the questions and answers, you can just fill in the points as you go.) Questions marked with an asterisk (*) are intended to assess the person's attitudes and are not scored, but there will be a place to summarize them on the Final Score Form.

Questions	Possible Points	Points Correct
1. Mary and John are coming home from a date. They like each other very much. Is it okay for them to hug?	*	*
2. Joe is home alone. Someone knocks at the door. What should he do? (1 point)	1	_____
3. Mary is sitting on the couch with Jane, her cousin. Is it okay for Jane to touch Mary's breast? (1 point). If it is not okay, whom could Mary tell? (1 point) What should Mary do if the first person she tells does not listen? (1 point)	3	_____
4. Jack is alone in his bedroom with the door closed. He is touching his penis. It feels good. Is this okay? (*) Do you know another word for this activity? (1 point)	* 1	* _____
5. Jean is alone in her bedroom with the door closed. She is touching her clitoris and vulva. It feels good. Is this okay? (*) Do you know another word for this activity? (1 point)	* 1	* _____
6. John is at work. He is rubbing his pants to make his penis feel good. Is this okay? (1 point)	1	_____
7. John is hitchhiking (getting a ride from a stranger). Is this okay? (1 point)	1	_____

Questions	Possible Points	Points Correct
8. Larry and Sam are homosexuals and love each other. Is it okay for them to touch each other's penis in private? (*)	*	*
9. Jenny and Marie are lesbians and love each other. Is it okay for them to touch each other's clitoris and vulva in private? (*)	*	*
10. Kate does not want Mike to pull her shirt. What should she do? (1 point)	1	_____
11. Mary lost her wallet. Her bus money was in it. What could she do? (1 point)	1	_____
12. John sees a new woman at his job? He wants to be friends with her. What could he do? (1 point)	1	_____
13. Mary is home alone and the phone rings. She answers the phone. The person on the phone starts saying nasty things to her. What should she do? (1 point)	1	_____
14. Liz is at work. Her boss, Mr. Smith, wants to kiss her What could Liz do? (1 point)	1	_____
15. These two people are boyfriend and girlfriend. They want to have sexual intercourse, but they don't want to have a baby. What should they do? (1 point)	1	_____
16. This woman just found out she is pregnant and she has told her husband. Tell me how she got pregnant. (1 point)	1	_____
17. Scott is the only passenger on the bus. The bus driver stops the bus. He sits by Scott and tells him he is cute. Then the bus driver asks Scott to touch his penis. What should Scott do? (1 point)	1	_____

Questions	Possible Points	Points Correct
18. What is this couple doing? (1 point)	1	_____
19. Using the drawing of the nude male and the nude female, ask the participant to identify various body parts on both the male and female and record responses using the charts below. (a) First, point to the body part and ask what the name is. (1 point each, 12 points total) (b) Second, name the body part and ask the person to point to it on the picture. (1 point each, 12 points total)	12 12	_____ _____

Question #19 MALE	(a) Correct	(a) Incorrect	(b) Correct	(b) Incorrect
Toes				
Neck				
Lips				
Thighs				
Penis				
Testicles				

Question #19 FEMALE	(a) Correct	(a) Incorrect	(b) Correct	(b) Incorrect
Chin				
Hips				
Eyebrow				
Pubic Hair				
Vulva				
Breast				

CORRECT ANSWERS for S.A.K. QUESTION/ANSWER FORM A

1. Attitude question (*)

2. Ask who it is before opening the door or don't open it if it is a stranger. (1 point)

3. No (1 point)
   She could tell a trustworthy person, such as a parent or teacher. (1 point)

4. Attitude question (*)
   Masturbation (1 point)

5. Attitude question (*)
   Masturbation (1 point)

6. No (1 point)

7. No (1 point)

8. Attitude question (*)

9. Attitude question (*)

10. Tell him stop or walk away (1 point)

11. She could talk to someone she trusts, such as the bus driver or a store clerk, or use the telephone to call someone such as a parent or staff person. (1 point)

12. Introduce him or ask her name. (1 point)

13. Hang up the phone. (1 point)

14. Tell him "no," or walk away. (1 point)

15. Use birth control, or name a specific contraceptive type such as condom or birth control pill. (1 point)

16. They had intercourse, or more specifically he put his penis in her vagina and the sperm met the egg. (1 point)

17. Say "no," or get off the bus. (1 point)

18. Having intercourse, or having sex (1 point)

FINAL SCORE FORM for S.A.K. QUESTION/ANSWER FORM A

For each question, locate the number listed below and transfer the score (# of correct points) from the Question/Answer Sheet. For attitude questions, summarize the person's answers in the blank under category (except for the Assertiveness section, where there are none). Note: Some of the questions are scored under more than one of the content areas.

UNDERSTANDING RELATIONSHIPS

Question #	Possible Points	Points Correct
3	3	
12	1	
14	1	
17	1	
Totals	6	

Summary of answers from attitude questions (#1, #8, and #9):

_____

_____

_____

_____

_____

_____

SOCIAL INTERACTION

Question #	Possible Points	Points Correct
6	1	
10	1	
12	1	
Totals	3	

Summary of answers from "attitude questions" (#1, #8, and #9):

_____

_____

_____

_____

_____

_____

SEXUAL AWARENESS

Question #	Possible Points	Points Correct
3	3	
4	1	
5	1	
15	1	
16	1	
18	1	
19	24	
Totals	32	

Summary of answers from attitude questions (#1, #4, #5, #8, and #9):

_____

_____

_____

_____

_____

_____

_____

_____

ASSERTIVENESS

Question #	Possible Points	Points Correct
2	1	
3	1	
7	1	
10	1	
11	1	
13	1	
14	1	
17	1	
Totals	8	

(No attitude questions)

S.A.K. QUESTION/ANSWER FORM B

For Individuals with Ability to Answer Yes/No Questions Only

After the questionnaire is completed, you can go back and check the participant's answers against the Correct Answers at the end of this form and record the points correct in the corresponding column. (Of course, if you are already familiar with the questions and answers, you can just fill in the points as you go.) Questions marked with an asterisk (*) are intended to assess the person's attitudes and are not scored, but there will be a place to summarize them on the Final Score Form.

Questions	YES	NO	Possible Points	Points Correct
1. Mary and John are coming home from a date. They like each other very much. Is it okay for them to hug? (*)			*	*
2. Joe is home alone. Someone knocks at the door. Joe looks out using the chain on the door and he decides that he does not know the person. Should he open the door? (1 point)			1	_____
3. Mary is sitting on the couch with Jane, her cousin. Is it okay for Jane to touch Mary's breast? (1 point)			1	_____
4. Jack is alone in his bedroom with the door closed. He is touching his penis. It feels good. Is this okay? (*)			*	*
Is masturbation another name for this activity? (1 point)			1	_____

S.T.A.R.S. © 2008 by Susan Heighway and Susan Kidd Webster. Future Horizons, Inc.

Questions	YES	NO	Possible Points	Points Correct
5. Jean is alone in her bedroom with the door closed. She is touching her clitoris and vulva. It feels good. Is this okay? (*)			*	*
Is masturbation another name for this activity? (1 point)			1	_____
6. John is at work. He is rubbing his pants to make his penis feel good. Is this okay? (1 point)			1	_____
7. John is hitchhiking (getting a ride from a stranger). Is this okay? (1 point)			1	_____
8. Larry and Sam are homosexuals and love each other. Is it okay for them to touch each other's penis in private? (*)			*	*
9. Jenny and Marie are lesbians and love each other. Is it okay for them to touch each other's clitoris and vulva in private? (*)			*	*

For the following questions, say the first statement, then ask each question. It may be necessary to repeat the first statement.

Questions	YES	NO	Possible Points	Points Correct
10. Kate does not want Mike to pull her shirt. First, should she: (3 Points)				
Tell him to stop?			1	_____
Kick him?			1	_____
Swear at him?			1	_____
11. Mary lost her billfold and her bus money was in it. What could she do? (3 points)				
Ask for money from a stranger at the bus stop?			1	_____
Look for a telephone to call home?			1	_____
Ask a community helper to assist her?			1	_____
12. John sees a new woman at his job. He wants to be friends with her. What would be best thing for him to say? (2 points)				
"Hey baby, want to go out for a date?"			1	_____
"Hello, my name is John, what's yours?"			1	_____
13. Mary is home alone and the phone rings. She answers the phone. The person on the phone starts saying nasty things to her. Should she: (2 Points)				
Hang up?			1	_____
Talk to the person?			1	_____
14. Liz is at work. Her boss, Mr. Smith, wants to kiss her. What could Liz do? (3 Points)				
Kiss him?			1	_____
Tell him "no"?			1	_____
Tell someone she trusts about what happened?			1	_____

Questions	YES	NO	Possible Points	Points Correct
15. These two people are boyfriend and girlfriend. They want to have sexual intercourse, but they don't want to have a baby. What should they do? (2 Points)				
They need to use birth control			1	_____
Don't worry about a pregnancy, because it won't happen if they have intercourse just one time.			1	_____
16. This woman just found out she is pregnant and she has told her husband. How did she get pregnant? (3 Points)				
She and her husband had intercourse and did not use birth control			1	_____
She ate too much watermelon			1	_____
She and her husband kissed a lot			1	_____
17. Scott is the only passenger on the bus. The bus driver stops the bus. He sits by Scott and tells him he is cute. Then the bus driver asks Scott to touch his penis. What should Scott do? (3 Points)				
Touch the driver's penis			1	_____
Comb his hair			1	_____
Get off the bus and tell someone he trusts what happened			1	_____
18. What is this couple doing? (3 Points)				
Are they wrestling?			1	_____
Are they having intercourse?			1	_____
Are they exercising?			1	_____
19. Using the drawing of the nude male and the nude female, ask the participant to identify various body parts on both the male and female. Name the body part and ask the person to point to it on the picture. Record responses using the charts below. (1 Point each, 12 points total)				

Question #19 MALE	Correct	Incorrect
Toes		
Neck		
Lips		
Thighs		
Penis		
Testicles		

Question #19 FEMALE	Correct	Incorrect
Chin		
Hips		
Eyebrow		
Pubic Hair		
Vulva		
Breast		

CORRECT ANSWERS for S.A.K. QUESTION/ANSWER FORM B

1. Attitude" question (*)

2. No (1 point)

3. No (1 point)

4. "Attitude" question (*)
   Yes (1 point)

5. "Attitude" question (*)
   Yes (1 point)

6. No (1 point)

7. No (1 point)

8. "Attitude" question (*)

9. "Attitude" question (*)

10. Yes (1 point)
    No (1 point)
    No (1 point)

11. No (1 point)
    Yes (1 point)
    Yes (1 point)

12. No (1 point)
    Yes (1 point)

13. Yes (1 point)
    No (1 point)

14. No (1 point)
    Yes (1 point)
    Yes (1 point)

15. Yes (1 point)
    No (1 point)

16. Yes (1 point)
    No (1 point)
    No (1 point)

17. No (1 point)
    No (1 point)
    Yes (1 point)

18. No (1 point)
    Yes (1 point)
    No (1 point)

FINAL SCORE FORM for S.A.K. QUESTION/ANSWER FORM B

For each question, locate the number listed below and transfer the score (# of correct points) from the Question/Answer Sheet. For attitude questions, summarize the person's answers in the blank under category (except for the Assertiveness section, where there are none). Note: Some of the questions are scored under more than one of the content areas.

UNDERSTANDING RELATIONSHIPS

Question	Possible Points	Points Correct
3	1	
12	2	
14	3	
17	3	
Totals	9	

Summary of answers from attitude questions (#1, #8, and #9):

_____

_____

_____

_____

_____

_____

SOCIAL INTERACTION

Question	Possible Points	Points Correct
6	1	
10	3	
12	1-2	
Totals	6	

Summary of answers from attitude questions (#1, #8, and #9):

_____

_____

_____

_____

_____

_____

SEXUAL AWARENESS

Question	Possible Points	Points Correct
3	1	
4	1	
5	1	
15	2	
16	3	
18	3	
19	12	
Totals	23	

Summary of answers from attitude questions (#1, #4, #5, #8, and #9):

_____

_____

_____

_____

_____

_____

_____

ASSERTIVENESS

Question	Possible Points	Points Correct
2	1	
3	1	
7	1	
10	3	
11	3	
13	2	
14	3	
17	3	
Totals	17	

(No attitude questions)

S.A.K. Question #1

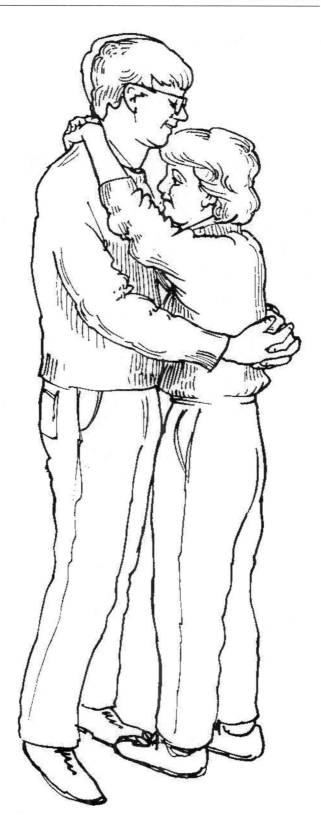

S.A.K. Question #2

S.A.K. Question #3

S.A.K. Question #4

S.T.A.R.S. © 2008 by Susan Heighway and Susan Kidd Webster. Future Horizons, Inc.

S.A.K. Question #5

S.A.K. Question #6

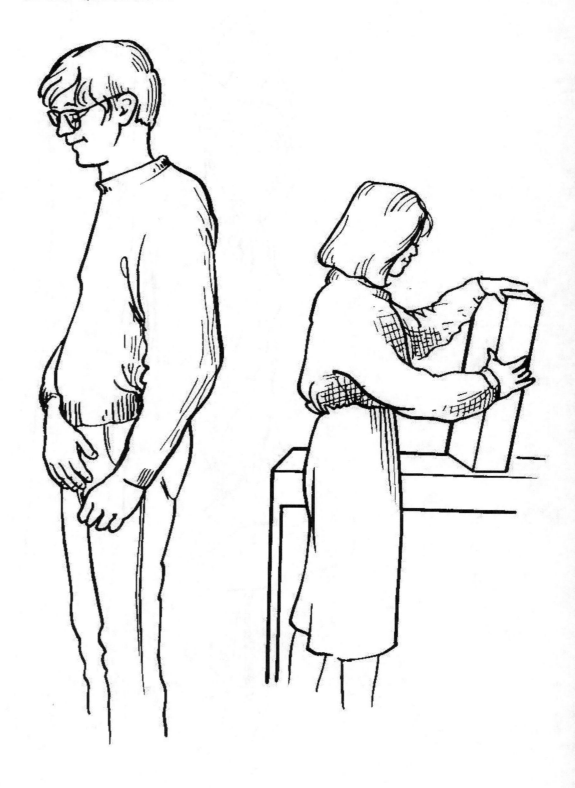

S.A.K. Question #7

S.A.K. Question #8

S.A.K. Question #9

S.A.K. Question #10

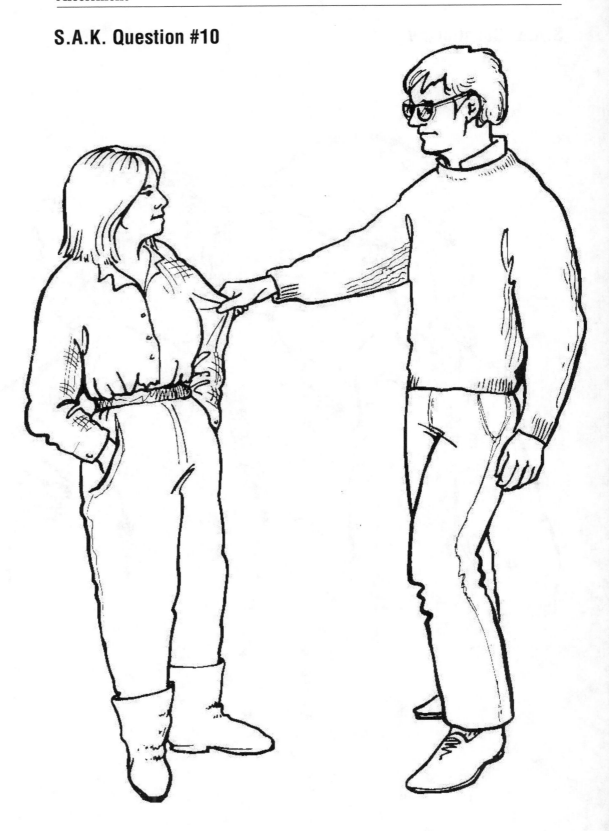

S.A.K. Question #11

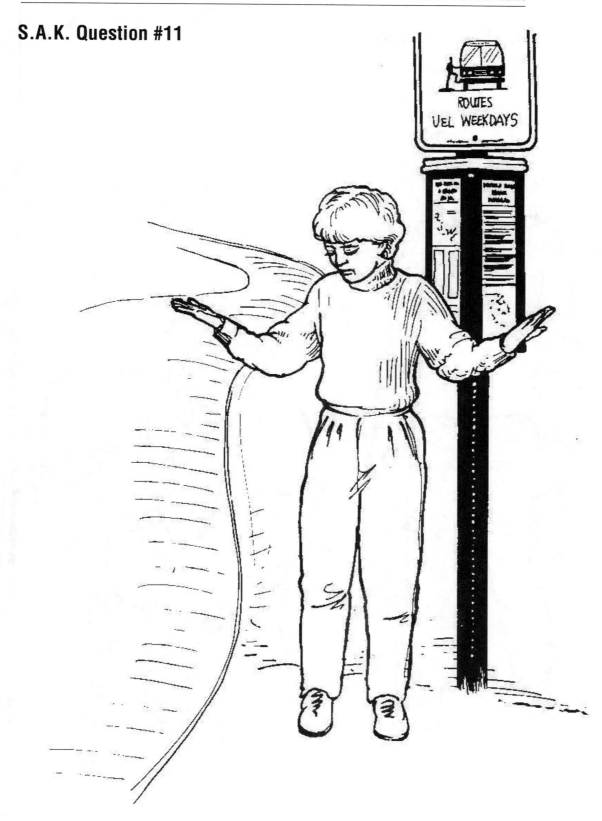

S.A.K. Question #12

S.A.K. Question #13

S.A.K. Question #14

S.A.K. Question #15

S.A.K. Question #16

S.T.A.R.S. © 2008 by Susan Heighway and Susan Kidd Webster. Future Horizons, Inc.

S.A.K. Question #17

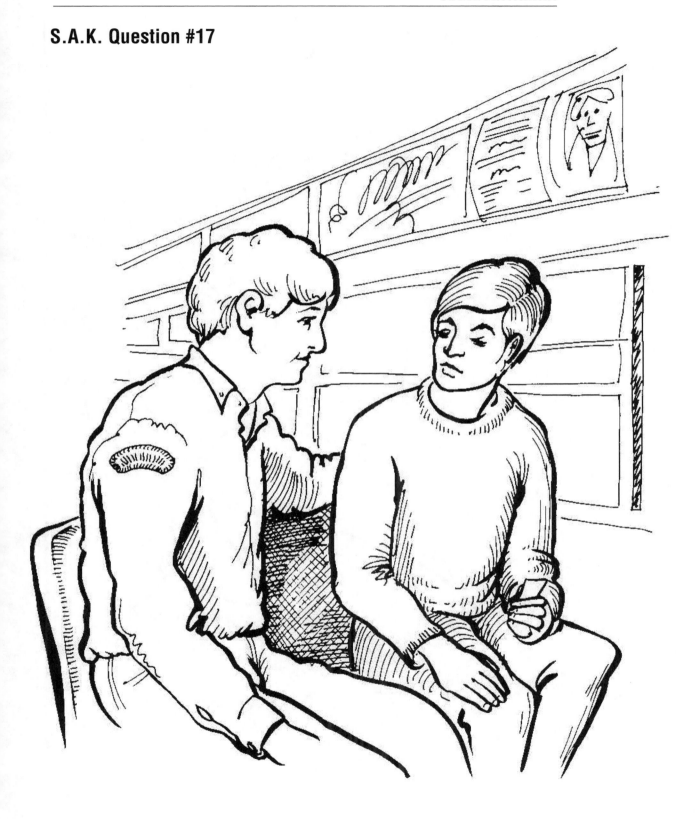

S.A.K. Question #18

S.A.K. Question #19
MALE

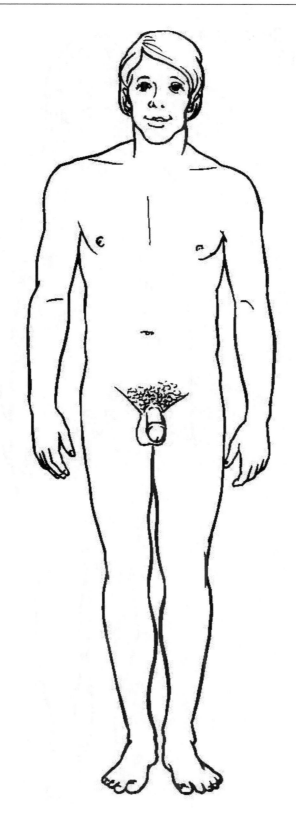

S.A.K. Question #19
FEMALE

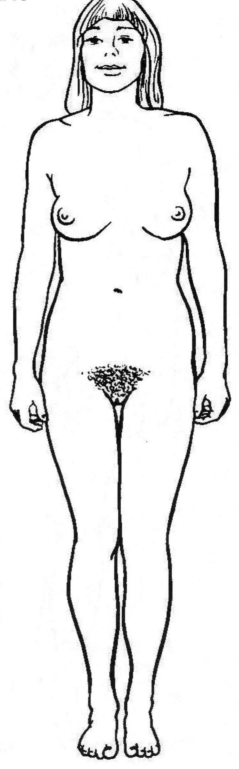

SEXUAL ABUSE RISKS ASSESSMENT (S.A.R.A.)

This tool can be used to identify situations or factors in the participant's life that may increase the individual's risks for abuse. It can be used to:

- Identify areas of concern where support, training, or intervention should be focused

- Address environmental issues that may contribute to the person's risk of abuse.

Things to consider:

1. If the trainer knows the participant well and is familiar with the individual's activities, relationships, and daily routines, then he/she may complete the assessment. If not, then the trainer should identify a person who is more familiar with the participant to be responsible for completing the assessment.

2. To the extent possible, the individual being assessed should be involved in the completion of the assessment.

3. The person completing the assessment may want to consult with significant others who know the person.

4. Some questions may not apply to the individual or may seem difficult to answer. It is acceptable to answer with "don't know" or "not applicable."

5. There is no formal scoring involved. We suggest that you mark questions with an asterisk (*) that raise issues around safety. If moderate or high risks are checked at the end of a setting section, mark this setting with an asterisk (*).

6. After completing the assessment, the trainer needs to carefully review the information in order to:

- Identify concerns that may increase risks for sexual abuse or prevent the development of positive sexuality

- Identify strengths and positive aspects in the participant's life settings and relationships.

This information, along with the results of the S.A.K., will be used in developing an Individual Training Plan (see form at the end of this section).

POINTS TO PONDER

- Supervised does not necessarily mean safe.

- Unsupervised does not necessarily mean unsafe.

- Group living does not necessarily mean safe.

- Independent living does not necessarily mean unsafe.

I. LIFE SETTINGS ASSESSMENT

This section can be used to assess the physical safety and security of the individual's environments and identify his/her settings as places that enhance or inhibit healthy expressions of sexuality. These settings include home, school, work, leisure/recreational settings, and other settings specific to the individual.

A. At Home

1. Describe the type of residence (e.g., foster home, group home, own home, adult family home, birth family, supported apartment, unsupported apartment, nursing home, institution).

   _____

   _____

2. Describe the location (e.g., residential neighborhood, business area, rural, isolated).

   _____

   _____

3. What is the size of the residence and the number of people living there?

   _____

   _____

4. Is the residence in good repair and adequately secured against intruders (e.g., adequate locks on doors and windows, is there a telephone or emergency call system)?

   _____

   _____

   _____

5. Is the residence arranged to respect the person's right to privacy? Are there private spaces?

_____

_____

_____

_____

6. Does the individual have his/her own bedroom?

_____

_____

7. If the person is in a group living situation, does the residential setting have a policy regarding sexual expression?

_____

- If so, what is it?

_____

_____

_____

_____

- Does the individual understand and agree with the policy?

_____

_____

- Do staff understand and agree with the policy?

  _____

  _____

- Do you think these policies enhance or inhibit expression of healthy sexuality?

  _____

  _____

  _____

  _____

8. Do you think the characteristics of the residence (e.g., location, daily schedule, and policies) support or inhibit the individual in developing friendships (with individuals who are not paid to be in the person's life) and close relationships? Explain.

   _____

   _____

   _____

   _____

9. Has the person or others ever expressed concern about safety in this setting? If yes, what is the nature of the unsafe feeling?

   _____

   _____

   _____

   _____

Describe concerns or suggestions for improving safety at home.

_____

_____

_____

_____

B. At School or Work

Use this to describe the person's out-of-home activities, such as participation in an educational program, employment, or volunteer placement. If a person spends time in more than one setting for these activities, be sure to provide the following info for each setting (forms for two settings are provided).

Work/School Setting #1

1. Describe the type of setting (e.g., public school, adult activity center, community job, sheltered workshop).

_____

_____

2. Besides staff, are there people in this setting who do not have disabilities?

_____

_____

3. Describe location (e.g., downtown, rural area, isolated area, business district).

_____

_____

4. What type of transportation does the person use to get to this setting?

_____

_____

5. What are the hours of training, employment, or volunteering?

_____

_____

6. Within the site, does the individual have isolated or private workspace, or does he/she work beside others? If isolated, are there other workers in the building or the area?

_____

_____

_____

_____

7. Does the setting have a stated policy regarding sexual expression and/or sexual behavior, and is the person aware of the policy?

_____

_____

_____

_____

8. Does the setting have a stated policy regarding sexual harassment? Is the individual aware of the policy and does he/she know how to report incidents?

_____

_____

_____

_____

_____

9. Does the setting foster building of social networks and friendships for the individual?

_____

_____

_____

_____

10. Has the individual ever expressed concern about safety in this setting? If yes, what is the nature of his/her concern?

_____

_____

_____

_____

Describe concerns or suggestions for improving safety at school or work.

_____

_____

_____

_____

Work/School Setting #2

1. Describe the type of setting (e.g., public school, adult activity center, community job, sheltered workshop).

   _____

   _____

2. Besides staff, are there people in this setting who do not have disabilities?

   _____

   _____

3. Describe location (e.g., downtown, rural area, isolated area, business district).

   _____

   _____

4. What type of transportation does the person use to get to this setting?

   _____

   _____

5. What are the hours of training, employment, or volunteering?

   _____

   _____

6. Within the site, does the individual have isolated or private workspace, or does he/she work beside others? If isolated, are there other workers in the building or the area?

   _____

_____

_____

_____

7. Does the setting have a stated policy regarding sexual expression and/or sexual behavior, and is the person aware of the policy?

_____

_____

_____

8. Does the setting have a stated policy regarding sexual harassment? Is the individual aware of the policy and does he/she know how to report incidents?

_____

_____

_____

9. Does the setting foster building of social networks and friendships for the individual?

_____

_____

_____

_____

10. Has the individual ever expressed concern about safety in this setting? If yes, what is the nature of his/her concern?

_____

_____

_____

_____

Describe concerns or suggestions for improving safety at school or work.

_____

_____

_____

_____

_____

C. Leisure/Recreational Settings

1. What does the individual typically do for leisure and recreation? List activities.

_____

_____

_____

_____

2. For each of the activities, complete a form below (forms for three settings are provided):

Activity:

_____

_____

Place:

_____

_____

Who is there?

_____

_____

What transportation does the individual use to get there?

_____

Does this activity provide an opportunity for interaction with persons who do have disabilities and who do not have disabilities?

_____

_____

Does this activity provide an opportunity for enhancing friendships and social relationships?

_____

_____

Has the individual or other people expressed any concerns about his/her safety in this setting?

_____

_____

Describe concerns or suggestions for improving safety in this setting.

_____

_____

_____

_____

_____

_____

149

Activity: _____

_____

_____

Place: _____

_____

_____

Who is there? _____

_____

_____

What transportation does the individual use to get there?_____

_____

Does this activity provide an opportunity for interaction with persons who do have disabilities and who do not have disabilities? _____

_____

_____

Does this activity provide an opportunity for enhancing friendships and social relationships? _____

_____

_____

S.T.A.R.S. © 2008 by Susan Heighway and Susan Kidd Webster. Future Horizons, Inc.

Has the individual or other people expressed any concerns about his/her safety in this setting? _____

_____

_____

Describe concerns or suggestions for improving safety in this setting.

_____

_____

_____

_____

_____

_____

Activity: _____

_____

_____

Place: _____

_____

_____

Who is there? _____

_____

_____

What transportation does the individual use to get there?_____

_____

Does this activity provide an opportunity for interaction with persons who do have disabilities and who do not have disabilities? _____

_____

_____

Does this activity provide an opportunity for enhancing friendships and social relationships? _____

_____

_____

Has the individual or other people expressed any concerns about his/her safety in this setting? _____

_____

_____

Describe concerns or suggestions for improving safety in this setting.

_____

_____

_____

_____

_____

D. Other Settings the Individual Frequents

(For example, the homes of relatives or friends, camp, respite, etc. Forms for three settings are provided.)

Describe the setting, including what the individual does there:

_____

_____

_____

_____

Who is there? _____

_____

_____

What transportation does the individual use to get there?_____

_____

Does this activity provide an opportunity for interaction with persons with and without disabilities? _____

_____

_____

Does this activity provide an opportunity for enhancing friendships and social relationships? _____

_____

_____

Has the individual or other people expressed any concerns about his/her safety in this setting? _____

_____

_____

Describe concerns or suggestions for improving safety in this setting.

_____

_____

_____

_____

_____

_____

Describe the setting, including what the individual does there:

_____

_____

_____

_____

Who is there? _____

_____

_____

What transportation does the individual use to get there?_____

_____

Does this activity provide an opportunity for interaction with persons with and without disabilities? _____

_____

_____

Does this activity provide an opportunity for enhancing friendships and social relationships? _____

_____

_____

Has the individual or other people expressed any concerns about his/her safety in this setting? _____

_____

_____

Describe concerns or suggestions for improving safety in this setting.

_____

_____

_____

_____

_____

Describe the setting, including what the individual does there:

_____

_____

_____

_____

Who is there? _____

_____

What transportation does the individual use to get there?_____

_____

Does this activity provide an opportunity for interaction with persons with and without disabilities? _____

_____

_____

Does this activity provide an opportunity for enhancing friendships and social relationships? _____

_____

_____

Has the individual or other people expressed any concerns about his/her safety in this setting? _____

_____

_____

Describe concerns or suggestions for improving safety in this setting.

_____

_____

_____

_____

_____

S.T.A.R.S. © 2008 by Susan Heighway and Susan Kidd Webster. Future Horizons, Inc.

II. RELATIONSHIPS ASSESSMENT

This section can be used to learn more about a person's social network and identify positive and/or challenging relationships. The best way to assure a person's safety is to make sure they have healthy relationships. Having a variety of people who care about the person minimizes risks for abuse or exploitation.

A. Family

Does the person have contact with family members? _____

_____

_____

With whom? _____

_____

_____

How often?_____

_____

_____

Does the person express positive regard toward family members?

_____

_____

_____

_____

Are there any concerns about these relationships? _____

_____

_____

_____

_____

_____

B. Friends (other than service providers)

Does the person have friends?_____

_____

_____

_____

A close friend? _____

_____

Any friends who do not have a disability?_____

_____

How often does he/she see these friends? _____

_____

_____

Does the person want more friends? _____

_____

_____

_____

Does the person date?_____

      One person? _____

      More than one person?_____

      Is this person in a steady relationship?_____

Are there any concerns about these relationships? _____

_____

_____

_____

_____

_____

_____

C. Service Providers

Most likely, this person is involved with numerous service providers (e.g., residential support providers, job coaches, social workers, health care providers, teachers, case managers, skill trainers).

Does the person need assistance from staff for basic physical care (e.g., dressing, bathing, or toileting)? _____

_____

_____

_____

Does the person have a staff person whom she/he can trust and confide in (e.g., someone the person would tell if something bad had happened)?

_____

_____

_____

Are there any concerns about these relationships? _____

_____

_____

_____

_____

_____

E. Other Significant Relationships

Describe any other significant relationships not covered above:

_____

_____

_____

_____

_____

Are there any concerns about these relationships? _____

_____

_____

_____

_____

_____

INDIVIDUAL TRAINING PLAN

Name of Participant: _____

Instructor: _____

I. Using information from the Sexual Attitudes and Knowledge Assessment (S.A.K.), complete this section to summarize any attitude, knowledge, or skill that causes concern, and suggest a plan.

Attitude, Knowledge, or Skill	Concerns	Plan for Focusing Training/Intervention/Support	Person Responsible

Strengths: _____

_____

_____

II. Using information from the Sexual Abuse Risks Assessment (S.A.R.A.), complete this section to summarize any setting or relationship that causes concern, and suggest a plan.

Setting or Relationship	Concerns	Plan for Focusing Training/Intervention/Support	Person Responsible

Strengths: _____

_____

_____

_____

Section Eight

Glossary

GLOSSARY

AIDS: Acquired Immunodeficiency Syndrome. AIDS is the final stage of HIV (Human Immunodeficiency Virus) infection. It can take years for a person infected with HIV to reach this stage, even without getting any treatment. Having AIDS means that the virus has weakened the immune system to the point at which the body has a difficult time fighting other infections. When a person has one or more serious infections and a low number of T cells (white blood cells that help the body fight off infections), he or she has AIDS.

Abortion: A surgical procedure done by a licensed physician (medical doctor) to end a pregnancy before the time when the baby would be grown enough to be born, usually during the first one to four months of pregnancy. Abortion is legal in the United States, although people have differing views on whether it is ethical or moral.

Anus: The opening that is the passageway for solid wastes (bowel movements, feces) that are in the intestines to be eliminated. Considered a private part and sometimes used for sexual activity.

Birth Control: Methods that are used if a heterosexual couple wants to have intercourse, but they want to prevent pregnancy. Also called contraception or family planning. There are several types of methods of birth control, including condoms and "The Pill."

Bladder: The organ, which is similar to a balloon or bag, inside the body that collects the urine.

Breasts: Both men and women have breasts, however, a woman's breasts grow larger than a man's breasts during puberty and can produce milk after childbirth. Breasts also are a source of sexual pleasure in most women and some men.

Cervix: The narrow, lower end of the uterus that has a small opening deep inside the vagina. This small opening, called the cervical opening, lets the menstrual fluid, or period come out; it also lets a man's sperm cells travel into the uterus and fallopian tubes. During childbirth, the cervical opening can stretch wide enough to let a baby pass through; after childbirth the cervix shrinks down to its normal size.

Clitoris: A small, sensitive organ in the woman, which is present solely for pleasure. The clitoris is about the size of a pea located in the soft folds of the skin that meet just above the urethra, at the top of the vulva. It has many nerve endings and is very sensitive. Pleasurable feelings result when the clitoris is touched during lovemaking, sexual intercourse, or masturbation. Stimulating the clitoris is the main way most women reach a climax, or orgasm.

Chancre: A very distinctive ulcer, which appears in the genital area or around the mouth. It is one of the first signs of syphilis, a sexually transmitted disease.

Chlamydia: A common type of sexually transmitted disease (STD). Males usually have symptoms that cause them to seek treatment. Females often do not have any symptoms and therefore do not seek treatment, which can lead to serious complications.

Climax: Also known as an orgasm. The height of sexual pleasure. Orgasm occurs after a build-up of sexual tension during lovemaking, sexual intercourse, or masturbation when there is a release, often somewhat sudden, followed by a feeling of well-being, or relaxation.

Condom: A birth control method first developed for men that is purchased in a pharmacy or drugstore in special packages. It is a sheath, or covering, worn over the erect penis during lovemaking or sexual intercourse to catch the semen when the male ejaculates. A condom is also used for "safer sex" to prevent the spread of sexually transmitted diseases. There is also a female condom, which is made to fit inside the vagina and over the labial folds.

Contraception: Birth control methods.

Discharge: An unusual white or yellow liquid that drips from a man's penis or comes out of a woman's vagina. It may mean that there is an infection.

Douching: A method to clean the vagina using special equipment (squirt bottle or douche bag) to squirt water or other liquid specially made for douching into the vagina. It is not effective to use for birth control.

Egg Cell: A tiny cell, which is the woman's reproductive cell. It is also called "an ovum" or "ova" (plural) that comes out of one of the woman's ovaries each month and travels down the Fallopian tube to the uterus. These eggs are very small, not the size of chicken eggs that we cook and eat, but so tiny that they are seen only with a microscope. If a man's sperm joins an egg cell, the egg and sperm together will grow into a baby.

Ejaculation: During intercourse or masturbation, sperm, or semen, squirt from a man's penis when an orgasm occurs (sometimes called, when a man "comes").

Erection: This happens to a man's penis when he gets sexually excited. The man's penis gets bigger and harder and it sticks out from the man's body.

Fertilization: When a man's sperm combines with an egg that is inside the woman's body. The fertilized egg attaches to the uterus wall and then grows into a fetus, or baby.

Genital Warts, Genital Herpes: Very common sexually transmitted diseases that are painful and difficult to treat. These diseases are caused by viruses.

Genitals: The name for the sex organs or sex parts that are on the outside of a man or woman. In a man, these are the penis, testicles, and scrotum. In females, they include the vulva, vagina, and clitoris.

Gonorrhea: A type of sexually transmitted disease that can be treated. It can be a serious problem, especially for women, because often symptoms are not obvious in females, so they might not seek treatment.

Heterosexuality: A sexual orientation in which a person has or wants to have sexual relations with a person of the opposite sex. That is, when a man has or wants to have sexual activity, including sexual intercourse, with a woman, or when a woman has or wants to have sexual activity, including sexual intercourse, with a man.

HIV: Stands for Human Immunodeficiency Virus. This is the virus that causes AIDS. HIV is different from other viruses because it attacks the white blood cells, an important part of the body's immune system. HIV damages the body's ability to fight other diseases, allowing serious infections to develop. HIV can be passed from one person to another, usually through intimate sexual contact or through sharing intravenous drug needles and/or syringes used for injecting drugs into the body.

Homosexuality: A sexual orientation in which the person has or wants to have sexual activity with a person of the same sex. That is, when a man has or wants to have sexual activity with a man, or when a woman has or wants to have sexual activity with a woman. Another name for homosexual is "gay." Homosexual women are also called lesbians.

HPV: Human papillomavirus is the name of a group of viruses that includes more than 100 different strains or types. More than thirty of these viruses are sexually transmitted, and they can infect the genital area of men and women. Most people who become infected with HPV will not have any symptoms and the infection will clear on its own. Some of these viruses are called "high-risk" types, and may cause abnormal Pap tests. They may also lead to cancer of the cervix, vulva, vagina, anus, or penis. Others are called "low-risk" types, and they may cause mild Pap test abnormalities or genital warts.

Masturbation: Rubbing or stroking the genitals for pleasure. Both men and women masturbate. It does not hurt. It feels good and is a healthy sexual behavior. It must be done only in private.

Menopause: A natural biological process, not a medical illness. Menopause is the time in a woman's life when her period stops because the ovaries stop producing the hormones estrogen and progesterone. It usually occurs naturally, most often after age forty-five. A woman has reached menopause when she has not had a period for one year. Changes and symptoms can start several years earlier.

Menstruation: A period. Blood and fluid come out of a woman's uterus through her vagina for a few days each month. It is necessary to wear a pad or tampon during the menstrual period. This begins during puberty.

Orgasm: The peak of sexual excitement for both males and females. See "climax" above.

Ovaries: Two very small sacks inside a woman's body that hold the tiny egg cells. Beginning in puberty, each month one egg leaves one ovary, then it goes down the Fallopian tube and into the uterus. The ovaries make the female hormones, estrogen and progesterone that regulate the menstrual cycle.

Pelvic Examination: A physical examination of the woman's internal and external sex organs by a doctor or nurse to make sure she is healthy. It usually includes a vaginal examination, using an instrument called a speculum, and a PAP smear (test for cancer cells) is also usually done.

Pelvic Inflammatory Disease: A serious type of sexually transmitted disease, which occurs in the female sexual organs, including the uterus, Fallopian tubes, and ovaries.

Penis: The man's sexual organ that hangs from the pelvic area. When a man gets sexually excited, the penis can become hard. Semen comes out of the penis when it is hard, and urine comes out of the penis when it is soft. During sexual intercourse between a man and woman, an erect penis is put in the woman's vagina. During masturbation, a man strokes or rubs his penis.

"The Pill": A highly effective method of birth control for women, if used properly. It is a pill that is swallowed and works by preventing ovulation (release of an egg).

Pubic Area: The place between the thighs in both women and men where the external genital organs are located. It is covered with "pubic hair" that starts to grow at puberty.

Puberty: A stage of human development during which both males and females develop into sexually mature adults, including secondary sexual characteristics and internal organs.

Prostate Gland: The part inside a man that makes most of the semen, the fluid that contains the sperm.

Rape: When a person is forced by another person to have sexual intercourse when he or she does not want to. Anyone who is raped should get help immediately. Contact a police officer and get help from a rape crisis center. Rape is a crime. It is one type of sexual assault.

Scrotum: The wrinkled sack of skin that hangs behind a man's penis. The scrotum holds the two testicles that make sperm.

Semen: The thick white liquid that comes out of a man's penis when he has a climax or orgasm. Sperm are in the semen.

Sex Organs: Another name for sexual body parts or genitalia.

Sexual Assault: Also called sexual abuse. It is any kind of forced or unwanted sexual contact between two persons, including touching sexual parts, sexual intercourse, or anal intercourse. There are many types of sexual assault: sexual contact with children by adults, incest, rape, same-sex assault, marital rape, and acquaintance or date rape.

Sexual Intercourse: The act of a man putting his penis into a woman's vagina. Pregnancy occurs through sexual intercourse. Usually intercourse is a sexual activity that occurs between two people who care about each other very much.

Sexually Transmitted Diseases (STDs): A group of diseases that people can get through sexual contact. These include many diseases ranging from mild to severe including gonorrhea, syphilis, genital warts, genital herpes, or HIV/AIDS. Currently there is also a varying availability of successful treatment for these diseases.

Sperm: Tiny reproductive cells made in a man's testicles. If one sperm meets with an egg from a woman's body, a baby will start to grow. Boys' testicles start making sperm cells sometime during adolescence.

Sterilization: A surgical procedure (closing off the sperm tubes, called *vas deferans* in the male, or closing off the fallopian tubes or removing the uterus in the female) which causes the male or female to be permanently incapable of conceiving or causing a pregnancy.

Testicles or Testes: Male reproductive glands located inside the scrotum. These glands make the sperm cells and a male hormone called testosterone. The testicles start making sperm cells sometime during adolescence and continue until old age.

Urethra: The tube that carries urine from the bladder to the outside of the body. Males urinate from the penis. Females urinate from the opening that is between the vagina and clitoris.

Uterus: This is a pear-shaped organ located at the end of the vagina inside the woman's abdomen. The lining of the uterus builds up each month in preparation for the egg. If the egg cell isn't fertilized, then the lining is shed about once a month and this is called menstruation. The uterus stretches to hold the developing fetus when a woman is pregnant, and shrinks down after the baby is born. Another name for uterus is "womb."

Vagina: This is an elastic-like passageway in a woman that leads from the uterus to outside the female body. It is the middle opening of the three openings inside a woman's vulva. Menstrual blood flows out of the uterus through the vagina to the outside of the woman's body. This is where a tampon fits during a period. The vagina can also stretch during childbirth to allow the baby to pass through. During intercourse, the penis is placed in the vagina.

Vulva: The genital organs on the outside of a woman's body, including the *mons pubis* (pad of fat tissue that covers the pubic bone), the *labia majora* (or outer lips of skin), the *labia minora* (or inner lips of skin), the clitoris, the urinary opening, and the vaginal opening.

Wet Dream: Ejaculation during sleep that occurs in adolescent boys and begins in puberty. It is normal, and boys cannot do anything to stop themselves from having them. Once they are through puberty, the dreams usually occur less frequently and then stop.

Section Nine

Resources

Resources

There are many available resources including curricula, books, videos, and other audiovisual aids to assist in the education of older adolescents and adults with developmental disabilities. Here is a list of resources about positive sexuality and abuse prevention that may be useful in your work.

PROGRAMS

Life Facts: Teacher Friendly Life Skills Program

This series includes information critical to independent living. The set of seven programs includes Sexuality, Sexual Abuse Prevention, AIDS, Managing Emotions, SmartTrust, Substance Abuse, and Managing Injuries and Illnesses. Features 11" x 14" laminated illustrations with lesson plans on the back. Available from James Stanfield Publishing Co., www.stanfield.com.

Life Horizons I: The Physiological and Emotional Aspects of Being Male & Female

This is a slide program widely used for sex education for persons with developmental and learning disabilities. The flexible slide format allows sexually explicit materials to be edited to meet student needs and community taste. *Life Horizons I* includes five programs with over 500 slides: Parts of the Body, Sexual Life Cycle, Human Reproduction, Birth Control or Regulation of Fertility, and Sexually Transmitted Diseases & AIDS. A comprehensive teacher's guide and one "Speaking of Sex" video are included. Available from James Stanfield Publishing Co., www.stanfield.com.

Life Horizons II: The Moral, Social and Legal Aspects of Sexuality

This slide program presents material on the psychosocial aspects of human sexuality with a focus on attitudes and behaviors that promote good relationships and responsible sexual behavior. *Life Horizons II* comes with seven slide programs, over 600 slides, and a comprehensive teacher's guide and script. Sections include: Building Self-Esteem & Establishing Relationships; Moral, Legal & Social Aspects of Sexual Behavior—Male; Moral, Legal & Social Aspects of Social Behavior—Female; Dating Skills & Learning to Love; Marriage & Other Lifestyles; Parenting; and Preventing or Coping with Sexual Abuse.

CIRCLES, Level 1: Intimacy & Relationships, Parts I and II

This is a teaching tool designed to help youths with cognitive limitations and difficulties with abstract concepts grasp the concepts of personal space, social distance and appropriate social/sexual behavior. The CIRCLES paradigm is used to teach social distance, and levels of familiarity, which are extremely abstract concepts, through the use of colored concentric circles. This program is designed to help students recognize exploitative relationships as well as develop mutually respectful ones. The connection between the kind of relationship and the corresponding level of intimacy is demonstrated visually, making learning easy for students. Part I: Social Distance is comprised of 11 video programs designed to help students "see" social and sexual distance, and explains the relationship between the level of intimacy between people and the way they touch, talk to, and trust each other. Students will learn relationship boundaries. In Part 2: Relationship Building, six video programs demonstrate how intimacy levels change as relationships change. The role of mutual choice among individuals is emphasized, a critical concept for protecting students from exploitation. The program comes with 12 video tapes, a 5' by 10' wall teaching graph, 50 large laminated graph icons, student "personal" graphs with 300 Peel 'n' Stick Icons, and one teacher's guide. Available from James Stanfield Publishing Co., www.stanfield.com.

CIRCLES, Level 2: Intimacy and Relationships

This is a follow-up program to *Circles Level 1* that shows how to apply the rules of social intimacy in more complex settings. It is a two-part video program. Part I: Recognizing and Reacting to Sexual Exploitation can be used to teach students how to recognize abusive behavior. Part II: Learning Appropriate Protective Behaviors includes real-life demonstrations of how to take positive action if feeling exploited. The program comes with three video tapes, a 5' by 10' wall graph, and one teacher's guide. Available from James Stanfield Publishing Co., www.stanfield.com.

CIRCLES, Level 3: Safer Ways—Aids and Communicable Disease Prevention

This two-part video program is used to present current information to students on avoiding and treating communicable diseases as well as ways to protect themselves against sexually transmitted diseases. Part I: Communicable Disease and Casual Contact is used to illustrate steps that can be taken to lessen the chances of catching a communicable disease. Part II: STDs, AIDS, and Intimate Contact promotes positive decision-making, including abstinence, to best avoid STDs and AIDS. Each program comes with both a general and explicit version of "How AIDS and STDs are Contracted" so the trainer can decide which level is most appropriate for the students and community. Also included are six video tapes, supplemental materials, and one comprehensive teacher's guide.

To order the above materials from the James Stanfield Publishing Co., or to request a catalog, contact:

James Stanfield Publishing Co.
Drawer 203
P.O. Box 41058
Santa Monica, CA 93140
Phone: (800) 421-6534
Fax: (805) 897-1187

Socialization and Sexuality: A Comprehensive Training Guide For Professionals Helping People with Disabilities that Hinder Learning
(1998) by Winifred Kempton

This encyclopedia of information on socialization and sexuality is an invaluable resource for special educators, teachers, psychologists, social workers, and parents. Content includes: Sexuality Education and Guidelines for Curriculum Design, Coping with Inappropriate Sexual Behavior, Sexual Abuse and Informed Consent, Working with Parents, Considerations Relating to Living Centers, and more. Available from Program Development Associates (info below).

VIDEOS/DVDs

Person to Person (DVD or VHS)

This is a 52-minute color educational video and discussion guide developed by Mary Ann Carmody, registered nurse, that will open communication about sexuality to parents, professionals, and persons with developmental disabilities. Both parents and their adult children talk about sexuality subjects related to menstruation, abuse, assertion, safety behavior, marriage, and AIDS. Available from Program Development Associates.

Walk in Our Shoes: Speaking Out About Sterilization (DVD or VHS)

Filmed in Australia, this emotionally charged program explores the ethics of whether or not, or in what circumstances, women and men with severe mental or physical disabilities should ever be sterilized. All parties involved desire a better quality of life for people who are believed to be incapable of fully comprehending, and then acting on, the issues for themselves. Candid interviews with parents, caregivers, members of the judiciary, and individuals with disabilities provide numerous angles on a topic that is as compelling as it is controversial. Available from Program Development Associates.

To order the above materials from the Program Development Associates, or to request a catalog, contact:

Program Development Associates
P.O. Box 2038
Syracuse, NY 13220-2038
http://pdassoc.com
Toll-free: (800) 543-2119
Fax: (315) 452-0710
Email: info@pdassoc.com

DVD Series on Relationships for People with Mental Retardation/ Developmental Disabilities

This DVD series, from YAI/National Institute for People with Disabilities, is helpful for teaching the abstract concepts of behavior in relationships. It includes: 1) The Friendships Series (3 parts), 2) The Boyfriend/Girlfriend Series (3 parts), and 3) The Sexuality Series (3 parts). See ordering info after next item.

Who Wants to Live for a Million Years? HIV/AIDS Prevention Interactive CD-ROM

Also from the YAI/National Institute for People with Disabilities, this CD-ROM can be used to teach HIV/AIDS prevention. Protecting oneself from

HIV and AIDS is an ongoing challenge for anyone, and for people with MR/DD, it can be especially challenging. Through this CD-ROM, users will learn some of the essential information and tools they will need to help keep them safe from HIV/AIDS infection. It will take the learners step by step from problems to solutions by allowing them to make mistakes while playing the game instead of in the outside world, where mistakes could lead to disaster.

To order the above materials from the YAI/National Institute for People with Disabilities, or to request a catalog, contact:

National Institute for People with Disabilities
Tapes and Publications
460 West 34th Street
New York, NY 10001-2382
(212) 273-6517
http://yai.org/trainingstore

BOOKS

An Easy Guide to Loving Carefully For Men and Women
(1987, Third Edition) by Lyn McKee, Winifred Kempton & Lynne Stiggall Miccigrosso

This guide provides a clear and uncomplicated presentation of facts about sexuality and reproduction. Simple illustrations on almost every page and a large type size makes this especially appropriate for people who have developmental disabilities. Available on Amazon.com.

Asperger's ... What Does It mean to Me?
(2000) by Catherine Faherty

This is a workbook explaining self-awareness and life lessons to youths with high-functioning autism or Asperger's Syndrome. Available from Future Horizons, www.FHautism.com.

Autism, Asperger's, and Sexuality: Puberty and Beyond
(2002) by Jerry Newport and Mary Newport

This book was written by a couple who were both diagnosed with Asperger's Syndrome as adults. It includes advice on dating, sex, birth control, disease prevention, abuse, and personal responsibility. Available from Future Horizons, www.FHautism.com.

Asperger's Syndrome and Sexuality: From Adoloescence through Adulthood
(2005) by Isabelle Henault

In this comprehensive and unique guide, the author delivers practical information and advice on issues such as puberty, sexual development, gender identity disorders, couples' therapy, guidelines for sex education programs, and maintaining sexual boundries. This book will prove indispensable to parents, teachers, counselors, and individuals with Asperger's Syndrome. Available from Jessica Kingsley Publishers, www.jkp.com.

Circles of Friends: People with Disabilities and Their Friends Enrich the Lives of One Another
(1988) by Robert Perske

This book offers true stories and issues to ponder concerning "circles of friends"—friendships between people with disabilities and non-disabled persons of all ages. Available from Inclusion Press International, www.inclusion.com.

Doing What Comes Naturally: Dispelling Myths and Fallacies about Sexuality and People with Developmental Disabilties
(2000) by Orieda Horn Anderson

A longtime sex educator who is still working well into her eighties, Orieda has created a compassionate and practical guide for social workers, counselors, families, and anyone who supports or cares about a person with developmental disabilties. The author addresses topics such as signs of sexual abuse, sexual incident reporting, and counseling techniques. She shares stories of success from people she has counseled. Available from High Tide Press, www.hightidepress.com.

Gay, Lesbian, Bisexual, and Transgender People with Developmental Disabilities and Mental Retardation: Stories of the Rainbow Support Group
(2003) by John D. Allen

In this book, the group founder John D. Allen describes the founding achievements and history of the Rainbow Support Group, a unique group providing

S.T.A.R.S. © 2008 by Susan Heighway and Susan Kidd Webster. Future Horizons, Inc.

support for GLBT people with developmental disabilties or mental retardation. Available from Haworth Press, www.haworthpress.com.

Informed Consent, Sexuality, and People with Developmental Disabilities: Strategies for Professional Decision-Making

(1996) by Laura Griffin, J.D., ARC Milwaukee, WI.

This workbook is intended to increase knowledge about sexual consent and decision-making for those who work with people with disabilities. Although the book often refers to the state of Wisconsin, the topic areas are relevant to all professionals.

Available from ARC Milwaukee, Inc.
7203 W. Center Street
Wauwatosa, WI 53210
Phone (414) 774-6255 Fax (414) 774-7859
information@arcmilwaukee.org

Navigating the Social World: A Curriculum for Individuals with Asperger's Syndrome, High-Functioning Autism, and Related Disorders

(2001) by Jeanette McAfee

This book offers a definitive program for developing social cognition, with forms, exercises, and guides for the student. It also presents significant educational guidance and supportive assistance to caregivers and teachers. Available from Future Horizons, Inc., www.FHautism.com.

The New Social Story Book Illustrated and Comic Strip Conversations

(2000) and (1994) by Carol Gray

The New Social Story Book is a programming resource that involves the development of simple stories in which the child is the main character and the other characters represent actual people in a real-life situation. Using visuals and carefully chosen words, it promotes social understanding and teaches communication skills for use in a wide variety of situations. The stories are good teaching tools for teaching positive social interaction.

A "Comic Strip Conversation" is a conversation between two or more people that incorporates the use of simple drawings. These drawings serve to illustrate ongoing communication, providing additional support to individuals who struggle to comprehend the quick exchange of information that can occur in a conversation. A basic set of symbols is used to illustrate social skills that are abstract and difficult for students with autism to understand.

Both books available from Future Horizons, Inc., www.FHautism.com.

Sex, Sexuality, and the Autism Spectrum
(2005) by Wendy Lawson

Written by an "insider," an openly gay autistic adult, Wendy Lawson writes frankly and honestly about autism, sex, and sexuality. After discussing basic sex education and autism, the author goes further to include wider issues such as interpersonal relationships, same-sex attraction, bisexuality, and transgender issues. She also examines the unspoken rules that exist between people in relationships and explains why these rules can be diffilcult and confusing for people with autism. Available from Jessica Kingsley Publishers, www.jkp.com.

Signs for Sexuality: A Resource Manual for Deaf and Hard of Hearing Individuals, their Families, and Professionals
(1991, Second Edition) by Marlyn Minken and Laurie Rosen-Ritt

This valuable manual contains more than 250 vocabulary terms associated with human sexuality and 600 photos showing signed words and phrases dealing with sexuality terms. Contains an appendix that includes descriptions of birth control methods, large female/male anatomy drawings, an introduction to sexuality education, and definitions of terms. This spiral-bound book lies flat, leaving hands free for signing. Available from Planned Parenthood, www.plannedparenthood.org/westernwashington/signs-for-sexuality-a-resource-manual-for-deaf-and-hard-of-hearing-individuals-their-families-and-professionals.htm.

Taking Care of Myself: A Hygiene, Puberty, and Personal Curriculum for Young People with Autism
(2003) by Mary Wrobel

Useful for teenagers and adults with autism spectrum disorders, this curriculum was specifically designed for students who are visually strong and capable of some physical manipulation of items. Using stories similar to Carol Gray's Social Stories, information in this book is prsented in a clear, simple way. Teaching topics include hygiene, health, modesty, physical development, menstruaton, touching, personal safety, and masturbation. Available from Future Horizons, Inc., www.FHautism.com.

Unwritten Rules for Social Relationships: Decoding Social Mysteries through the Unique Perspectives of Autism
(2006) by Temple Grandin and Sean Barron

This enlightening and thought-provoking book educates those on the spectrum and their caregivers about surviving and thriving in the social world. Having been diagnosed with autism themselves, Temple and Sean lead you through their mistakes and the ways they found to improve their lives. Available from Future Horizons, Inc., www.FHautism.com.

ORGANIZATIONS AND RESOURCE CENTERS

CDC National Prevention Information Network (NPIN)
www.cdcnpin.org

This is a United States reference, referral, and distribution service for information on HIV/AIDS, STDs, and tuberculosis. NPIN produces, collects, catalogs, processes, stocks, and disseminates materials and information on the above topics to organizations and people working in those disease fields in international, national, state, and local settings.

Maurice Ritz Resource Center and Planned Parenthood of Wisconsin, Inc.

302 North Jackson Street
Milwaukee, WI 53202
(414) 289-3704 or (800) 472-2703
Email: library@ppwi.org

This community library and bookstore features one of the largest collections on human sexuality and sexuality education in the Midwest. There is an extensive collection of resources specifically related to disability and sexuality.

The National Women's Health Information Center (NWHIC)

www.4women.gov

> NWHIC is a service of the Office on Women's Health (OWH) in the US Department of Health and Human Services (HHS). It is the most reliable and up-to-date information resource on women's health today. Free women's health information is offered on more than 800 topics through the call center and website.

Planned Parenthood Federation of America

www.plannedparenthood.org

> This website is the official gateway to the online Planned Parenthood community and to a wealth of reproductive health and rights information, including numerous services and resources. Planned Parenthood believes in the fundamental right of each individual, throughout the world, to manage his or her own fertility, regardless of the individual's income, marital status, race, ethnicity, sexual orientation, age, national origin, or residence. The goal of Planned Parenthood is to ensure that sexuality is understood as an essential, lifelong aspect of being human, and that it is celebrated with respect, openness, and maturity.

The Sexuality Information and Education Council of the United States (SIECUS)

www.siecus.org

> SIECUS affirms that sexuality is a fundamental part of being human, one that is worthy of dignity and respect. SIECUS provides information and training opportunities for educators, health professionals, parents, and communities across the country to ensure that people of all ages, cultures, and backgrounds receive high quality, comprehensive education about sexuality.

COMMUNITY RESOURCES

The following are agencies in your local community or state which may be helpful in developing a sexuality training program for people with developmental disabilities:

Rape Crisis Centers

State Councils on Developmental Disabilities

Public Health Departments

Family Planning Agencies

Association for Retarded Citizens

AIDS Support Networks

RESOURCES FOR SAFE USE OF THE INTERNET

Online Safety Tips from Microsoft

www.microsoft.com/protect/family

Internet Safety: Safe Surfing Tips for Teens

http://kidshealth.org/teen/safety/safebasics/internet_safety.html

Several Safety Articles about Blogging, Social Networking Sites, and More

www.safeteens.com